SURVIVING WAR, SURVIVING AUTISM

A Mother's Life Story

D1416487

Kim Yen Nguyen, PharmD

Best Wishes ~
Kim Yen

Surviving War, Surviving Autism: A Mother's Life Story

ISBN: 978-1-61170-052-7

Printed in the USA and UK on acid-free paper

For additional copies of this book go to:
www.rp-author.com/knguyen

 **Robertson Publishing**™
59 North Santa Cruz Avenue
Los Gatos, California 95030 USA
www.RobertsonPublishing.com

DEDICATION

This book is dedicated to my children and to all individuals and families living with autism. I also dedicate this book to my father, who instilled in me the courage and resilience to overcome unimaginable hardships with amazing hope and strength. I hope it will make a positive impact on anyone who has been through challenging and difficult times in their lives. If I can bring hope and inspiration to just one person, one family, writing and publishing this book will have been well worth the effort.

A portion of the book proceeds will go towards various organizations that help individuals and families affected by autism as well as those performing research into the causes, prevention, treatments, and cure for autism. Among these are Autism Speaks, Autism Society of America, and Parents Helping Parents. In addition, this book will also benefit the many programs and schools that have contributed so much to the well-being of my children over the years.

TABLE OF CONTENTS

PREFACE

When I came to the United States at the age of thirteen in 1975, I thought my tumultuous journey was over. I'd left the winds of war behind me. The waves of death and destruction had spared me. The turbulent storm had stopped swirling around me, and I stepped on new land with renewed hope and a dream. Little did I realize then that I was about to embark on another long and arduous journey full of hardships and challenges. I rely on the best of my recollections to recount for you the people, places and events that have shaped my life and strengthened my resolve to persevere despite the circumstances. Sometimes the passage of time fades the details of these memories, but the spirit and emotion of the time remain as vivid as the bright colors of a Van Gogh painting.

Throughout the years filled perhaps with more tears than cheers, my faith, love and devotion to my children sustained me and allowed me to overcome even the biggest hurdles and the darkest of days. Sometimes I searched for answers when none existed, and I wanted to find causes when the effect was that of a greater cause.

What is autism? Autism is a neurological disorder that affects an individual's ability to communicate and interact with others. Signs and symptoms usually begin in early childhood — before the age of three. The affected child generally displays a delay in or a regression from achieving developmental milestones, such as crawling, walking, speaking, cognition, and interaction with others. Common characteristics may include speech and language delay, social impairment, eye contact difficulty, repetition of words or phrases made by others (echolalia), an aversion to change, triggered outbursts, constant rocking or body motion, and obsessive interests. The exact causes of autism are unknown at this time. Although autism is not curable, with early diagnosis and intervention, autism is treatable.

Autism does not discriminate. The disorder strikes those from North America, South America, Europe, the Middle East, Asia, or Africa. It affects people who are Black, Caucasian, Asian, Latino, mixed race, rich, and poor. Yes, autism affects people of all races and cultures. Autism is a global disease, thus it needs global attention. The Centers for Disease Control and Prevention (CDC) website reports that autism now affects one in every 110 American children. Previously, it affected one in every 150 children. This would indicate that autism may constitute a national health crisis. Despite advances in research, no cure exists for autism at the moment. We now know that early recognition, early intervention, and early treatment help autistic children in reducing their symptoms and improving their chances of living and functioning to the fullest of their ability.

I am a single mother raising three children all diagnosed with autism at different ages and with different degrees of severity. It should be noted that I was an engineer turned housewife and mother and, more recently, a housewife and mother turned pharmacist; the life experiences I recount here come from the perspective of a mother rather than from the viewpoint of an engineer or a pharmacist. I have been through a living hell at times to help my children get to where they are now — to help them live with their autism, but they still have a long way to go. I will continue to help and support them every step of the way.

By sharing my personal story and experiences, I hope to help other families of children with autism and to inspire many who face such difficult challenges in the United States and around the world. If heartache or affliction has touched your life in any way, may you find some comfort, hope, and inspiration in these pages.

CHAPTER 1

THE BEGINNING – GROWING UP

DURING THE WAR

I start at the beginning of the storm.

I grew up in a small rural area in southern Vietnam, where I spent much of my childhood running from the waves of gunfire, bombings, and destruction. My traumatic experiences of the Vietnam War and its impact pale in comparison to those suffered in the aftermath of the fall of Saigon and the postwar era and to those who survived the dangerous sea journey to the United States. But that part of my life — that tiny portion of the Vietnam War as seen through the prism of memories of a child growing up during the war — serves as an important part of my past. That early chapter of my life, my childhood, contains so many sad stories I could not recount them all, and, truth be told, I would rather forget most of them. Yet, these experiences strengthened my resolve and helped me overcome the unexpected challenges and hardships I encountered years later.

I was seven years old when the Tet Offensive began on January 31, 1968. This attack by the communist forces of the People's Army of Vietnam against those of the Republic of Vietnam (South Vietnam) and its allies was particularly significant, because it occurred on the Lunar New Year holiday, at a time when all of Vietnam should have been celebrating. So many times we had to go underground and sleep overnight in a small, dark tunnel-like hiding place to avoid the bombings and artillery fire. Everyone, including the children, was supposed to be still and quiet. I remember one time I slept so soundly underground, I didn't realize the mosquito incense had burned a big hole on my sleeve overnight but amazingly had spared my skin. The next morning many families with small children returned home. My mom also took us back to our house, which was located several hundred yards from the underground place. Exhausted, worried, and confused, we walked like zombies down a well-trodden dirt path lined with sandy stones and dried withering grass.

As my mom opened the door, I felt an icy chill run down through my spine. Bullet holes riddled the walls, pictures and other items were scattered on the floor, and the house seemed as if someone had ransacked it. We stood there oblivious to the occasional sound of distant gunfire or explosions. After all, last night was one of the worst nights of battle and we had slept through it; that's how immune we had become to the sounds of war. My mom told us to be careful of the broken glass on the floor. We stayed only long enough to pick up some clothing and personal items, but in that short time something happened…and I could not erase nor forget what happened next no matter how hard I tried. Even these many years have not dulled the memory.

Out of the window, I heard the screaming, hysterical voice of an old woman, which I later recognized as one of our great aunts. She seemed distraught and devastated as she mumbled something about somebody passing away. My mom went out and tried to console her, but she didn't stop crying. After a while, my great aunt walked away and disappeared behind the bushes. When my mom came back inside, we all asked curiously, "Mom, what happened?" The silence was deafening; we waited anxiously for my mom's response. She started to sob, but I could still hear what she said. One of our relatives, a six-year-old boy who liked to perform magic, had been playing in the yard with other kids when he saw a can of Coke. "He picked it up," she explained. "There was a grenade inside." She sobbed before continuing. "His face was blown up beyond recognition...and he is dead." She said and buried her face in her hands.

He was just only a year younger than I was at the time. Six-year-old kids are not supposed to think about life and death let alone succumbing to such a tragic death so suddenly at such a young age. I was numb. I kept repeating, "Why?"

The war had claimed one more life in addition to the many lives lost on the battlefield, at school, in the market, in the office building, in the theater, at home, and now, in the front yard where children were supposed to play on swings and with toys. It had been so dark in that underground tunnel last night, but I wondered if he had been one of the boys sharing the same underground hiding place with me. He had escaped the bombings and artillery only to fall to the most innocent act — his final act, his final curtain call — picking up a can of Coke? I felt a sense of gut-wrenching emptiness, sadness, and disgust. I thought about war and its impact. I wondered why people could not coexist peacefully. I wondered why some people would have to use a weapon to pierce someone's heart and mind to make a point.

The clouds of fear and uncertainty of growing up in the war, the sadness and suffering of every family directly or indirectly touched by the casualties of war are immeasurable. I couldn't tell you how much we suffered either, but I could see the effects of the war on my family. During that period, I remember seeing my mom crying on numerous occasions because one of our friends or relatives had died in the war. Every so often, I saw a funeral pass our house casting a gloomy pallor over the whole family. The war felt particularly difficult for us since my father was serving as a soldier in the South Vietnamese Army. A mine almost killed him; fortunately, he escaped with serious injuries and, after a long hospital stay, was honorably discharged back to our family. To say that we were relieved would be a grave understatement.

After the Tet Offensive, my father packed our entire family, which included my mother, seven children, and my uncle, on a Lambretta as we tried to move from a small province in the rural countryside to Saigon without disobeying the ongoing curfew. Even now, I do not know how he did it, but we all managed to fit snugly on that small scooter. My mom held the baby, and my sisters, brothers and I all held on to the sides around our dad and towards the back of the scooter. Our vehicle was one of the very few on that route. Along the way, my father had to stop at the various designated checkpoints because of the curfew. The soldiers were nice and sympathetic to us; they chatted with my father, who was a former army captain, and inspected our Lambretta. Then they allowed us to pass.

There were times my father told us to close our eyes as we bumped along on the scooter. The first time, young and curious as I was, when he said, "All of you close your eyes now and don't open them until I say so," I peeked to see why. I wished I had listened to him. I saw corpses lined up on the side of the road. I remember the breeze rushing past my face, but I felt like I was suffocating. I gasped for air — fresh air that is. The next time, I closed my eyes and imagined some funny thoughts. I daydreamed about being a singer on stage wearing my mom's high-heeled shoes and accidentally falling and landing on my bottom. The whole audience was laughing, and I laughed, too.

The smile on my face diminished suddenly as the loud popping sounds of gunfire brought me back to reality. Apparently, some stray bullets barely missed our Lambretta. My youngest sister started to scream, and at first, I thought that the bullets had struck her.

"It's okay!" my mom assured us. "The loud gunfire just startled her and woke her up. She didn't get hit." I breathed a sigh of relief. Every moment seemed like an eternity after that. I felt as if the winds of war were closing in and, at any minute, might become a hurricane that swirled each of us apart and in different directions. I wished I could wave the magic wand and make the war go away, but I could only close my eyes and pray hard every time I heard sounds of gunfire or artillery. I am sure my parents were also praying. Someone from above must have heard our prayers.

We finally made it to Saigon safely. Thereafter, we moved quite often, either staying with relatives or renting one place after another in or near Saigon. We did not have much money, but we were happy that we had each other. There were many Vietnamese Tết (Lunar New Year) holidays after that, but for me, and perhaps for those who experienced the Tet Offensive, 1968 was the most significant New Year — simply beyond words.

I remember one place where we settled for a few years. My mom usually worked with my grandmother at the market pretty far from where we lived. Thus, my siblings and I stayed mostly with babysitters. I spent most of my childhood with my brothers and sisters — to be exact, three brothers and five sisters. Since we moved so frequently, I rarely had close friends. This was the first time I was able to develop a few good friends from the neighborhood.

One day I asked my mother if I could go to the movies with the other girls. "No," she said adamantly. "Sometimes people put grenades and bombs in the movie theaters. I'm afraid you could get hurt…You can't go."

In the mornings, after my parents left for work, my older sister and I took turns working the makeshift street mini-market selling edibles such as tomatoes, mushrooms, eggs, and various vegetables. In the afternoons, I attended school. Though deep down inside I always believed many people have goodness within them and, regardless of the circumstances, there are good and bad people everywhere, maybe it was just my luck that I met quite a few not-so-nice people while growing up.

For instance, one day I had to study for an exam and came late to the mini-market, thus I had to settle my egg basket in a small corner in front of a house. The street vendors lined up on both sides of the street and claimed good spots on a first come, first served basis. I was careful not to block the driveway of this particular home. Everything seemed ordinary, and I was able to sell several dozen eggs when suddenly I heard the loud shrieking voice of a woman yelling profanities at me from inside the house. Before I could get up and move this angry woman appeared on her front porch holding a toddler's hand. They both stepped down from the porch.

For some unknown reason, she pushed her son on top of my egg basket. As she picked up her crying son, whose hip was drenched with the egg wash, she pushed me to the side and quickly took my money from a small can. Then she pointed her finger at me and yelled, "Move or I'll hit you hard!"

The commotion caused some vendors to gather around, but they did not interfere or say anything. One of them muttered, "She's just a kid, just forgive her this time." I carried my dripping egg basket with more than a dozen broken, damaged eggs, and hurriedly ran home. I was embarrassed, to say the least, but I was also so terrified of her that I wanted to cry, but the tears did not come. As I ran, my fear of the woman turned to worry about what to tell my mother about the money and the eggs. If I told her about the whole incident, would she believe me? She would probably think I tripped and damaged the eggs or used the money to buy candy.

I don't remember what I told my mother or how she reacted. What I do remember is that as I made my way home I repeatedly told myself I would never bully a kid. I would never be like that woman.

From this point on in my childhood, a few events stand out in my memory. They remain imprinted in my mind as short vignettes, not even full stories. I remember I enjoyed school and worked diligently. I considered myself an average or above average student at best. At that time, I was just a simple kid with big dreams of becoming a singer or an actress and having a family. I remembered writing letters to a few famous singers and actresses only to have those letters returned to me because I accidentally addressed them to myself.

Some of my friends and classmates from Trung Vuong High School, where I attended 6th, 7th, and 8th grade, later came to America, as did I. My eyes teared up, and I was overcome with joy and emotion years later when we got a chance to see each other again. They were all so nice and lovely. It was such an amazing coincidence to run into one of my former classmates at the same IBM location where we both worked. Trung Vuong High School held so many beautiful memories and friendships for me, and I was able to revisit them every time we were reunited with one another.

Since we lived far from school, my sisters and I rode the bus there every day. After stepping off the bus, we walked down the narrow roads and alleys that sometimes were littered with garbage, bottles, glasses, cockroaches, and even dead mice. Nothing seemed to bother us; we talked and laughed all the way home. I remember an exception to this time of laughter; I recall that I cried because a saw a group of kids bully a boy whose only crime was that he had a cleft foot and walked unevenly.

Memories come back to me also through the things I still enjoy, reminiscent of my time in Vietnam. I still love Vietnamese food and music. When I was about four years old, I told myself one of my goals would be to learn to read and write — and I did so by reading and writing song lyrics I heard from the radio. By the time I reached the age of 12, my many papers with song lyrics cluttered the house. This upset my mom, and one day she threw out most of them. I sang Vietnamese songs for my younger baby sisters and rocked them to sleep in a hammock. Sometimes, my sisters and I put a short musical together, and we performed songs for several kids in the neighborhood. I even used my own allowance to buy cookies ("banh men") for them.

For the most part, the rest of my recollections of Vietnam appear as flashbacks or just bits and pieces of memories. When someone in the neighborhood threw a stone at my sister's eye, I felt devastated because I thought she would lose her eyesight in that eye. One time, my brother fell down a long flight of stairs. My mom wrapped him in a blood-soaked towel and frantically ran out to get a taxi to take him to the hospital. On a hot and humid summer afternoon, a fire broke out in our rented house that nearly killed my sisters and me.

Then there are the people… One of my elderly great aunts came to live with us for a while. I recall fondly my grandmother and uncles who visited us and gave us lucky money, "li xi," as presents for the New Year. One of the babysitters told me if I sat and ate so close to the old television, it would explode, and the "bad people from the television" would come out and get me. For many years after that, I was worried and always sat far away from the television.

One of my clearest memories comes from a special mentor and teacher from my childhood, one of the nicest people I had the good fortune of knowing in Vietnam. She was tall and thin with a strong northern accent and shoulder-length hair. After helping me with homework, we played tic-tac-toe games. It seemed either I was lucky or she was just being nice, but I won close to one hundred games. At that time one of my siblings was a bratty child and said mean things to her. Nevertheless, I remember her kindly telling me, "Kim, I will keep coming and will help you because you work hard and have the potential to succeed."

A few days before my birthday, she asked my mom if she could organize a birthday party for me. At the time, it was the sweetest thing anyone had ever done for me. She baked a cake and made a pyramid out of sugar cane. She put a red orchid in my hair and told me I looked like a "princess." It was a simple birthday with no fancy food, no fancy balloons or decorations, no fancy presents, but that precious moment will forever remain in my mind. To this day, I will never forget her. It was the best and the only birthday celebration I ever had in Vietnam. We moved shortly after that, and I never got a chance to see saw her again. If I ever have the opportunity to go back to Vietnam to visit my relatives and friends, I certainly will look for her and thank her.

One of the last things I remember from growing up in Vietnam was the loud arguments and profanities that would emanate from the house across the street from us. Kids, mostly boys, would gather in front of the windows and watch like a spectator sport as the husband beat his wife. Most of the time, no one bothered to intervene. Perhaps it was common at that time that some husbands had mistresses, got drunk, gambled, and the wives either endured in silence or spoke up and get beaten up. Perhaps it was common that the women bore the burden of taking care of the family — husband and children — physically, psychologically, and sometimes even financially.

When this happened, I thought about my father. *How lucky for my mom and for us that my father is not part of the norm. He does not smoke, drink, or have mistresses. He even helps my mom by taking care of*

8

us when my mom has to go somewhere. My sisters and I always enjoyed his cooking and singing when my mom wasn't around. I have seen my parents arguing many times, but I have never seen my father hit my mom even once. Even though spanking children is common in Vietnamese culture, he rarely spanked us. If we did something wrong, he would always tell us not to do it again. If we did, we'd have to add up the amount we owed him from this time and next time, and that could result in a long spanking.

My father taught us to love and care for one another, and most of all, he taught each of us to be good people — no matter what situations we encountered in life. If there is one thing I remember most from my childhood in Vietnam and beyond, it is this: *My father's priority in life has always been his family and children.* That is the blessing that God, or Buddha, has given us.

CHAPTER 2

THE TUMULTUOUS JOURNEY

TO AMERICA

My family life changed dramatically a few years later when we not only moved again but half our family relocated to a different city. When my father started a new job, he and three children (including me) rented a new place, and the three of us children continued to attend Trung Vuong High School in Saigon. We took the bus to school every day, and we usually came back to this tiny rented room before our father returned from work.

The owner did not allow us to cook, so we bought food from a nearby market instead. One time, my father gave us money to buy "pho," a popular Vietnamese rice noodle soup, for dinner. Unfortunately, two portions had cockroaches along with the noodles. He gave us his portion and did not eat anything that night.

My mother and the rest of the children resided in Vung Tau, a seaport city in Vietnam. Weekends, breaks and in the summer we got a chance to go to Vung Tau and see our siblings. My brothers and sisters really enjoyed swimming and playing on the beach. I can close my eyes today and still picture the panoramic ocean vista and its breathtaking beauty, especially during sunrises and sunsets. Too soon, I would be taking my last footsteps on the sands of Vung Tau.

My mom had hoped to begin a small shrimping business from Vung Tau. In the early spring of 1975, my parents purchased a small boat that could be used for commercial fishing. They hired an operator for this boat, a strong stout man with a deep voice and menacing look. Nevertheless, on April 28, 1975, he would be the one to navigate the boat that would take us to our new life in a new country. His wife behaved nicely toward my mom but unkindly to her stepson, who was a couple of years younger than me. I felt bad for him and many times, I tried to console him.

I did not know all the details or the reasons why we had to board this fishing boat that fateful April day. I overheard bits and pieces from my mom, but I really didn't understand. Days later, with the presence of the Americans, I began to fathom the significance of this journey. A major life changing event was happening right before my eyes, and I realized I was leaving everything I'd ever known behind.

I remember feeling nauseated and claustrophobic after I first set foot on this 3.5 m x 16 m fishing boat. Yet, I was amazed at how many people, adults and children, could be crammed onto this boat: the operator's family, which included his wife and several children, and our family, which included my parents and ten children. My youngest sister was only sixteen months old. In addition, I saw several boxes of varying shapes and sizes containing the personal belongings of both families.

The next few harrowing days on the Pacific Ocean left an incredible imprint in my mind. Most of the children including me became seasick, vomiting constantly the first day. All the children huddled in a small corner of the boat, with the older kids taking care of the younger kids (an unspoken rule in our culture). I was in and out of consciousness, feeling so sick I could hardly eat or drink anything.

The second day, we encountered a thunder storm with heavy rain, dark clouds, and turbulent waves that rocked the boat wildly back and forth. I shivered and curled up in a fetal position with my hands over my ears as each deafening crack of thunder arrived after the brightness of the lightning. Then I noticed a commotion. The

11

adults were yelling about a leak in the boat, and my parents began scooping out the water with a small pail.

Our boat was small against the vast Pacific Ocean and definitely not well equipped for the long difficult journey. Our clothes became damp and drenched from the sea mist and the rain, only to dry and become soaked again intermittently in a cyclical fashion. My parents also began to throw overboard many of our boxes of personal items and clothing in an effort to lighten the boat. The waves pounded away at the boat, and at times it felt like the boat would be smashed apart. Surprisingly, it showed tremendous resilience and continued to float, albeit unsteadily.

I forgot exactly at what time of the day, but I imagined it must be later in the afternoon or closer to the evening, when I heard the loud sounds of gunfire. My eyes squeezed shut, and my body stiffened with fear; I will always associate this sound with war and death. I repeatedly told myself I was dreaming.

A few minutes later, one of my younger sisters started to cry and asked for something to drink. I reached over to where I knew there was a cup and discovered it overflowing with water from the rain. I gave her the cup and said, "Be quiet." I didn't want her to wake the others.

Her voice trembling, she responded, "Look...There is a man with a gun."

At first, I thought she either was joking or hallucinating. Then I opened my eyes wide and looked in the direction of her finger. I saw a man, wearing a soldier's uniform and carrying a gun jump to our boat from another boat. At the same time he was talking to the operator of the boat. There was some exchange between my parents, the soldier, and the operator of the boat, but I could not hear exactly what was said. Then I heard the soldier asking that our boat turn back to pick up some additional passengers. My parents continued scooping water from the boat while the operator talked to him. My sister and I watched in fear as he walked closer and closer to us. I saw the long barrel of his gun pointed downward and sometimes sideways. I wondered which death would be quicker, drowning or dying from a gunshot wound.

The soldier started to examine our leaky boat. He saw water seeping in from the bottom of the boat and recognized that the boat could sink anytime, especially given the heavy rain and stormy weather. He immediately signaled to another boat nearby by shooting his gun up in the sky, and eventually he jumped ship and left us alone.

That night the storm came again, and my parents continued to scoop as much water out of our leaky boat as they could. They were exhausted and hopeless when the sun finally came out in the early morning. In fact, we were all worn-out, dazed, and tired. Some of us were quietly praying and clinging on to the hope that a miracle would happen. I looked down; there was water everywhere around our feet and the bottom of the boat. I looked up, and although the rainfall would continue again mildly, still more and more water piled into our small and shaky vessel...

I thought of myself then as a thin girl, struggling with an immense force, who eventually would be lost at sea. I thought about the swirling waves and tumultuous tides that would sweep all of us somewhere underneath the Pacific Ocean. I also thought about other inherent and imminent dangers: snacks for sharks or prey for pirates. We all knew it was only a matter of time before the boat capsized.

Yet destiny is just as powerful as the thunderstorm at sea or the tide of terror that sweeps the lives of those who risk everything in search of freedom. Someone above had a different plan for us. I had sat curled up in a ball, assuming the worst scenario would come to pass, when my parents both came to find my siblings and me. "Come see!" they said, and my father put his hand on my shoulder. "We are about to be rescued by a U.S. fleet!" With joy and relief, I jumped up and ran to the railing. Sure enough, there was a large American boat—the most beautiful ship I had ever seen – an impressive and strong grey fortress on the Pacific Ocean.

First, we had to climb up from our boat to a "xa lan," which resembled a big barge with high walls. I remember climbing up the high wall and then jumping down into this barge with no shoes on. *Ouch!* I thought as I landed. In the chaos lay a plan: The big kids

climbed in first to catch the younger kids as they jumped or whatever personal things were thrown over that we could take from the
boat. My mother stayed with the small kids to prevent them from
falling into the ocean. My father climbed up with one of the small
kids in his arm. He then quickly passed the child to me or to my
older sister and rushed back to get another one. Even though we
were weak and exhausted, somehow we managed to climb into the
xa lan with vigor, our renewed hope and adrenaline sustaining our
energy. Looking around, so many people from other small boats
that had congregated towards this xa lan were doing the same
thing: trying to climb and cling on to hope.

I remember catching one of my younger siblings first as well as
a very big heavy box from the fishing boat operator's wife. "Be
careful!" she had yelled as she threw it at me. The box was so heavy
it almost crushed my face and chest. In fact, the weight of this box
caused me to stagger and gasp for air. Later I discovered bruises on
my arms and fingers from trying to clutch it and found out that box
contained her television. It dawned on me that while my parents
threw most of our boxes including our personal clothing to the
ocean to lighten up the boat, the boat operator's wife never parted
with any of her "valuable" things.

I vaguely remembered the logistics. A group of people processed paperwork for all the families in the xa lan. Each family
eventually got transported in a mesh-like basket or container up to
the big ship after the paperwork was completed. Our family was
one of the last groups leaving the xa lan. While waiting for the
transport, someone heard a rumor that the ship was already filled
to capacity; thus, people crammed into that netted basket every
time it came down to load more passengers. The commotion started
again when someone threw a bottle, and glass shattered on the
ground. Barefoot with no shoes or thongs, as I walked I tried to
avoid the glass and other litter, an activity that added to my exhaustion. Luckily, my mom later found a pair of worn-out thongs
that someone threw away for me to wear. I smiled gratefully at her
as I put them on my feet.

We finally settled onto the U.S. boat. Each family built a make-shift dwelling spot on the big ship on a first come, first serve basis. Since we came close to being last, ours was a small uncovered area on the top deck. Using a translator, the Americans told us the ship was sailing toward the Philippines, where we would stay temporarily. Our next destination was Guam and then Camp Pendleton, California, where we would await our sponsor – an individual or a group in the United States that pledged to receive and assist in the care of a refugee family. I guessed the government needed time processing all the paperwork as well as finding sponsors for all the refugees.

The next couple of days on the ocean brought relief and joy to all my brothers and sisters. My seasickness was subsiding, the rain stopped, and I started to enjoy the breeze and the calm of the Pacific. As I stood on deck watching the incoming and outgoing waves, I couldn't help thinking about our past, present, and future. Almost everything seemed like a wave, moving up and down, and at times, standing still amidst the chaos. I saw each of us as just tiny particles on that wave, not knowing what the next move would be or where it would take us. The same wave that brought terror days ago now brought calmness and serenity. This seemed surreal to me. Yet, as I watched the waves my panic subsided; the face of despair morphed into the face of determination.

Having reached relative safety, my parents felt mixed emotion. They were happy we escaped the chaos of the fall of Saigon and the threat of communism, but they also felt sad and worried about the fate of other friends and relatives in Vietnam. They continued to worry about the uncertainty of their future and that of their ten children. While talking about America, my mom mentioned our uncle, the only relative we had at that time who was already in America. The fact that we knew someone there somehow felt comforting and gave us faith that we soon could reach our destination. We were all eager to meet him.

Since there were so many of us on a ship that probably was caught off-guard and not prepared for such a large-scale rescue operation, food supplies were rationed. Every day, we only received one small portion of food (apples, bread, etc). My parents always saved most of their portions for us children.

It was sunny and breezy during the day, but it was cold at night on the ship. Someone gave us a couple of blankets, and we all huddled together under them. My brothers and sisters were very compliant, but they were confused and puzzled. A few of them asked, "When are we going home?" No one could answer that. Not even my parents. We didn't have a home or a country anymore. We only had each other, and we all felt grateful.

With a whole new life before me, I thought a bit about what I wanted. *It would be nice to have a lot of money and wealth, but it's much more rewarding and fulfilling to be surrounded with the warmth and love of a family, an ordinary family. In the end, happiness is the only thing that lasts — the only eternal thing that we can carry with us. That's enough for me,* I concluded. No more dreams of singing and acting on a stage.

The days on the ship went by quickly. Someone told our family we were approaching the Philippines. After we got off the ship, each of us got a spray of DDT, which at that time smelled like perfume to me. We were also given military clothing, quite a bit long and large for our sizes, but we loved it. It was better than our dirty worn out clothes. Then we got in a very long line for what seemed like good, fancy food (mostly military canned food). All of us children became gluttons overnight. We ate so much and even tried to hoard bananas and apples. We had finally set foot on land once again and gotten a good meal even if it was on paper plates and eaten with plastic spoons, forks, and paper napkins. It seemed like a banquet to us. After being on a fishing boat that nearly capsized and on the xa lan waiting to board the big ship, then being on the ship for several days, the Philippines seemed like heaven.

The U.S. government then flew us to Guam for a couple of days and after that off to Camp Pendleton, a U.S. Marine base located north of San Diego. Upon our arrival at Camp Pendleton, there was more paperwork to process. Our family was assigned a tent with army cots; our temporary "home" located a distance up a long and winding dirt path near a group of tall trees. We lived in that tent for several weeks in Camp Pendleton while waiting for an American sponsor. It was quite chilly at night, and the children got sick with colds quite often. At night, my mom walked around each cot to make sure we were all covered in blankets.

Sometimes my sisters and I picked up fallen twigs and played tic-tac-toe games right on the dirt just below our cot. We didn't need much to have fun. I had learned some simple English phrases and sentences from textbooks during my last couple of school years in Vietnam, but the trauma of the boat journey erased most of what I had learned. I had forgotten all but a few common words.

During the day, we stood in long lines for food and learned some basic spoken English as well as American culture from volunteers. One day, one of my younger sisters came back from lunch and excitedly reported, "Guess what, it's just like in the book! I said, 'Hi, how are you?' And the Americans responded."

I ventured out a bit and met a courteous, kind-hearted American volunteer, Ms. C.S., who taught me some English. She had no children and wanted to adopt me. One of the reasons I wanted to be adopted was to help my family and expedite the sponsoring process. Although my English was still severely lacking, in many of our fragmented conversation, she and I shared joy and laughter at times. I began to form a strong friendship toward Ms. C.S., and I will always treasure that. Unfortunately, things did not work out.

We were a big family, thus finding a sponsor for us would not be easy. We felt happy for the other families who left the "Tent City" after getting a sponsor and wished our turn would be next. Finally, after many weeks of longing and waiting, we received a sponsor, not from California but from Texas. We left the sheltered existence at Camp Pendleton for Texas in what would be a rough awakening into a different culture, tempered with the grace and acceptance of a Southern community.

CHAPTER 3

TEXAS – THE TRANSITION

We arrived in San Antonio, Texas, in the midst of a hot and humid summer in 1975. Our sponsor met us at the airport and drove us a long way to a small town called Uvalde near San Antonio. However, we did not stay there long. Our first sponsor owned a vacation rental spot with lots of cabins in a deserted wooded area. We stayed in one of his cabins. I guessed his intentions were for our big family to help him with his business. Every day my father would do yard work, mowing lawns and trimming bushes. The big kids helped with cleaning up cabins after the guests checked out. Most of the time, I cleaned the cabins with my mom or sisters, but sometimes I would clean one cabin all by myself, especially when there were many guests. After cleaning up the toilet, changing the sheets, and vacuuming the room, I would be tired. I would head for the refrigerator or the counter top to see if the guests had left any food. Sometimes I was lucky and found plenty of sandwiches, chips, and pickles. Other times, I was not so lucky, and discovered only empty beer cans, bottles, and cigarettes butts.

I also remembered practicing my English with the guests there. I would be so brave and waive and say "hi" to them. Then, after they said something else, I would stand stunned and unable to respond because I had no idea what they had said. I would run as fast as I could back to the cabin and cry; I wished I knew more English.

18

Some of the guests were nice and friendly to us. They actually ventured to our cabin and greeted us, "Hi, how are you?" I supposed they were curious to see an Oriental family with ten young children living in a cabin in the woods.

We did not leave the property much. A few times a group of nice people came by and took us to see a school very far away. But it was too far away, and the wheels were set in motion to figure out the logistics of getting us there on a daily basis. So, we waited.

We did not receive any wages for our work, but our sponsor did supply us with food from the convenience store he and his wife ran. They had a daughter about my age and a small baby. The daughter worked hard at the chores, but she was cordial and friendly. Although my English was so limited, we talked and laughed together occasionally.

Our sponsor treated us nicely, but being a family with ten young children in a secluded area with no money, little communication, and no transportation and being dependent upon another posed many challenges. When my brother fell and badly hurt his head and our sponsor did not take my brother to the doctor, my parents were upset and contacted our uncle. He complained to some agency that eventually arranged for us to move and for a new sponsor.

Our second sponsor was St. Mark's Episcopal Church in San Antonio, whose members were kind and generous and assisted us in the transition to our second home in America. They helped us rent a house via the housing program, even provided furniture, clothing, and appliances through donations. With the church's help, we got a small used car, and the children were registered with the local school district. My father began working as a janitor at the church, and my mom stayed home to take care of my younger brothers and sisters. We were all baptized and given godparents. Our godparents were very kind to us, and even though we've long since moved, we've kept in touch with some of them over the years.

The summer following our move to San Antonio, my older sister and I were given a chance to attend the church summer camp. We had never been to a summer camp, and we had a wonderful experience. Since we did not have any nice summer clothes, the Church volunteers took us to a fancy store and bought us adequate essentials. During that summer, we learned to read the Bible and sing hymns. We even put on a skit and performed songs for the group. One beautiful starry summer night, all the children shared stories and enjoyed roasting marshmallows together.

At Memorial High School in San Antonio, the first school in America that I attended, I noticed early on that some students were rowdy, smoked, hugged and kissed their friends right in front of the teacher, wore heavy make-up, and had more freedom to do what they wanted in class, including talking back to the teacher. Almost the entire student body, as well as the teachers and staff, spoke Spanish, which made life a bit more difficult for my older sister and me since we were barely able to understand English. They could have teased us or bullied us — after all, we are the new kids in town who not only looked different but also talked differently and could not understand English, let alone Spanish. On the contrary, they were nice to us, welcomed us, and helped us feel at home. I loved the students, the teachers, and the staff there and the fact that the school was situated atop a scenic hill.

The staff assigned me to the 9th grade, since they asked me what grade I was in Vietnam, and I replied the 8th grade. I had an extremely difficult time at first adjusting to the new environment, new location, new school, new classes, new culture, and the language. Every day after finishing my household chores of sweeping, cleaning, and washing dishes, I stayed up late into the night trying to use the English/Vietnamese dictionary to help with the translation for my homework assignments. Eventually, though, using the dictionary to do my homework became too overbearing and exhausting. After school, I asked the teachers for help, especially with my English.

I knew learning English and getting comfortable with my studies would be a long road, and the challenges seemed never ending. Nevertheless, I fell in love with the school, the teachers, the people, the culture, the food, and the music of my new home in Texas. Even our first trip to the supermarket brought tears of joy to my eyes. *In the land of plenty, no one should go hungry,* I thought — *there is just so much food.* My first English I exam, my first grade in Algebra I, my first World History map, my first speech in Speech & Drama class, and everything was just different and amazing. All of my teachers were supportive, helpful, and understanding. They even organized my fifteenth birthday party!

Sometimes I was overwhelmed with lots of homework and asked my dad for help. I did not want to bother him much because he had to wake up very early and worked hard until late afternoon. Then when he came home, he always tried to fix things around the house — a broken faucet, a hole in the screen door, a clogged sink, or an overflowing toilet. One time, I asked him, "Dad, what is the difference between beautiful and bountiful?"

He looked up the words in the dictionary and tried to explain to me. Then he told me something in Vietnamese I will never ever forget. He said, "Remember…when you are bountiful, you're beautiful inside and out. That's the difference."

I am grateful to have a wonderful father who has taught his children so much and sacrificed so much for them. As we grew up, each of us individually may not have made the best decisions, and collectively we caused him much pain, but he never complained or put us down. Regardless of how each of us turned out, he has done a superb job of being a father.

Although I enjoyed all my academic classes at Memorial High School, I dreaded going to physical education (PE) class. Not only was I slow at running, I did not know how to play any sports, such as volleyball or basketball. Therefore, I was hit by the ball many times. My PE teacher, Mrs. A., realized this, and she took extra effort to ensure that other kids did not bully or harass me in any way. One day, while playing soccer, a girl kicked the ball, and it hit me square in the calf. I was hurt badly and started to cry. My teacher let me sit on the sidelines. I felt sad, so I comforted myself by singing a song to myself. A girl heard me singing; she waved to her friends, and suddenly they all gathered around to hear me sing. After that, often instead of playing sports, I just sang Vietnamese songs for the class. Even though they did not understand the lyrics, they seemed to enjoy listening to the tones and the melodies.

During a baseball game in PE class, it took me 17 times to strike a ball. I did not know the "three strikes and you're out" rule, so I continued to try repeatedly until I hit the ball. My patient PE teacher allowed me to keep on trying on a hot and humid afternoon on the field.

To this day I also feel indebted to my English teacher, Mrs. M., for helping me with the transition and making a significant difference in my life. Once, I did not know what the word "jump" meant, and in her high-heeled shoes, she jumped up and down to show me. One day, after class, I came to see her because I was so frustrated with a reading in a book chapter and trying to understand what each word meant. Even if I tried hard to use the dictionary for translation, I still did not understand the theme, plot, and characters. "Stay positive and don't give up, Kim," I can still hear her saying to me. Then she taught me different ways to approach the problem. She used simple examples, things to which I could relate and words easy for me to understand. By the time we finished reading a few pages, it was already dark. She offered to take me home so I didn't have to walk to the bus station. At home, I was able to finish reading the chapter. Even though I did not understand all the words, I could identify the major characters, the protagonist and antagonist, and the plot. The next day I checked with her to see if I had gotten these things right. "I'm so proud of you," she said as she confirmed that I had, indeed, done the homework correctly.

One day I arrived late to English class because the bus was delayed, and everyone in the class looked at me and chanted "Tardy...Detention..." I did not know what these words meant until my English teacher explained to me. In fact, I was happy to have "Tardy" and "Detention" because I loved to come after school to see her. This teacher cared so much about me she even took me to the doctor when I was sick.

My World History teacher, Mr. C., always encouraged me. These were his exact words: "In America, if you work hard, you can be anything you want to be." He lectured mostly in Spanish, but when he saw that I was confused, he immediately switched to English. He told me I should never be afraid to ask for help and never afraid to ask questions, no matter how stupid the questions might be. I took his advice literally. One day it was raining heavily, and we could not walk to the bus stop. I didn't know what to do, and I called him. He drove to our place and actually gave all of us a ride to our schools, including dropping off my younger brothers and sisters at the middle school and elementary school. I thought how lucky the opportunity to have him as a teacher and mentor. His words and deeds of kindness still encourage me to this day.

Math was the only subject I did not struggle with much. At first, the counselor placed me at a lower math level. I really didn't learn anything, and I wanted to change classes but did not know how to ask for this. Out of frustration, a few times I started crying in class. One student asked me why, but I didn't know how to explain my frustration. Then one day, she told me that if I didn't like this class I could always change to a different one. I looked at her as if she was my savior, and I nodded my head to indicate, yes, indeed, I wanted to change classes. She brought me to the office to initiate the change.

The school officials gave me a few tests, and I was able to pass them, so they allowed me to change midway to accelerated Algebra I. I was much happier in this class, and an interesting thing happened in there as well. One girl told me that she had a crush on Mr. V., my Algebra I teacher. I was so afraid for my teacher; I thought she was going to "crush" him physically. Someone later explained to me what "having a crush" really means.

The principal came to my English I class and discussed graduation requirements. At that time, Memorial High School was under the quarter system. The principal wrote the required courses on the board, the number of quarters needed per course, and then she tallied the total number of quarters needed for graduation. Now I can't recall the exact number she put on the board. For the sake of argument, let us say that the number she mentioned was 60 quarters. The principal then asked, "Do you all want to graduate? Raise your hand if you want to graduate." The entire class raised their hands. "Good. I want to see each and every one of you with 60 quarters." Even though I did not know what "graduate" meant, I also raised my hand since the whole class seemed excited to "graduate."

I came home that day and asked my parents for 60 quarters. They were puzzled. I told them that the principal required each of us to have that many quarters. They did not have enough quarters so they borrowed from the neighbors. The next day, I showed up at the office with the exact number of quarters. The principal was not there, so I showed it to another office staff member. I'm sure they wanted to laugh out loud, but they didn't. What a way to learn that the same word in the English language can have two different meanings. Tricky language!

One of my most beautiful high school memories comes from a lesson I learned from my Speech & Drama teacher, Mrs. A. At first, I felt intimidated to stand up and talk because I had such poor English and possessed a strong accent. My teacher encouraged me, though, and made me feel brave. She gave me advice on what to say, how to say it, and even when to say something. Then we practiced repeatedly. She saw in me the innocent but dedicated little girl who worked hard, enjoyed learning, and put tremendous effort into school. One time, a boy in the class was making fun of my language, and she called him aside and talked to him. After that, he never teased me again.

At the end of the year, she and I put together a musical program, called "From Vietnam with Love," in which we sang and danced Vietnamese songs on stage in the auditorium. It was my way of thanking the teachers, students, and staff here for welcoming my family into their school, helping us to feel at home, and teaching us the value of hard work and the lessons of kindness and compassion. My Speech & Drama teacher handled all the logistics: the permission, the program, flyers, stage, and lights, and I coordinated everything else: singing, background music, dancing, and costumes. The cast also included my sisters and other Vietnamese students. After each rehearsal, my teacher would take us to Dairy

Queen, and we ate ice cream. Life was as sweet as those cones, and I wanted it to last forever.

On the day of the performance, my teacher introduced the program and performers but suddenly handed me the microphone. I could not believe it! Surprisingly, I spoke coherently in front of that large audience (even though it was impromptu and the butterflies were beating, not fluttering their wings inside me). I even managed to introduce a few important guests and thanked the teachers, students, and staff. The experience was exhilarating.

My father, who had a cast on his arm due to injury sustained earlier in the week, sat in the front row with the important guests. He smiled constantly and was so proud to see his children on stage singing and dancing. My Speech & Drama teacher later told me I should pursue singing and dancing — and she didn't even know this had once been my dream!

The brownstone-like building in San Antonio that we called home was a bit small and became even smaller as we welcomed another baby, my youngest sister, to the family. She would be the first and last American-born child for my parents. We also shared our house with a prolific family of cockroaches. I remembered opening one of the cabinets and screaming because several cockroaches fell right onto my face. Soon enough, we learned to co-exist. Where else would we go? I think sometimes our resident bugs thought we were over-running the place. Nighttime would find some of us kids asleep on the couch, some on the bed, and some on the floor. My sister and I found a place to sleep on the floor near the furnace because it was warm there.

Everyday my mother cooked and fed us mostly rice dishes and packages of noodles, much like what we ate in Vietnam and conveniently affordable with our limited budget. However, we also were beginning to explore and expand our taste of American and Mexican food. We had very little money, so it was always a treat when my mom bought tacos at Taco Bell or hamburgers at McDonald's. Two of us shared one taco, and two or sometimes three of us shared a hamburger or a hot dog. We rarely fought each other over food or clothing. I believe all of us were overwhelmed, amused, and amazed at the new culture, new school, and new environment. We did not have much, but we were happy and grateful for what we did have.

San Antonio brought so many new experiences and challenges to this bewildered teenager. I didn't know how to use a locker and always had difficulty with mine, so I kept bringing many books home every day. I walked quite a distance from the high school to the bus stop, and it was difficult to carry those heavy books.

Sometimes I felt uncomfortable and experienced pain when I urinated. I shared this fact with a friend, who told me I might have a urinary tract infection (UTI). I didn't know what it was, but she told me I might need to see a doctor.

I didn't know how to see a doctor in America. I did not know I had to call and make an appointment. I remembered opening the Yellow Pages and looking for a doctor with an easy last name, like Brown or Blue or Red. I could not find any doctor with the last names Red or Blue, but I did find one with Brown. I did not know what to do, so I started writing a letter to this doctor. A few days later, I received a phone call from his receptionist giving me an appointment.

My English teacher gave me a ride to the doctor's office on the day of my appointment. It turned out that I did not have UTI, but the pressure exerted against the lower part of my stomach by the heavy books I had been carrying was just too much for me. I therefore had to ask my teachers if I could leave the books in the classrooms for days that I did not have homework. Sometimes I worked during lunch to finish my homework, so I wouldn't have to carry those books home later.

The next year we moved to another house, also in San Antonio, but in a different school district. The owner of this house normally did not accept the government housing program, but he was generous and made an exception. The house was nicer, larger, and had fewer cockroaches. My sister and I went to a new school, Lanier High School.

I remember my uncle came for a short visit. He helped my sisters and me with our homework. Afterward, we talked and laughed for hours. I was so excited about the new high school and the new culture in which we were immersed that every day after school I could not wait to go home and tell him everything. I was just a kid back then, and I thought of him as not only my uncle but also as my friend. He was there for me then, and I am grateful for that fact. Many years have passed; many things have changed, but our conversations remain comforting memories.

Although the teachers at this school were more reserved and strict than the teachers at Memorial High School, they welcomed my sister and me and helped us whenever we needed it. I was in the 10th grade, and my sister was in the 11th grade. I remembered attending Typing I class, and feeling intimidated because I previously had never learned to type. It seemed everyone here was much better at typing than me. After class I asked the teacher if I could come in during the last period and practice typing. My teacher agreed. I felt bad because while she was teaching a class, I kept on practicing and typing away in the back of the classroom. Eventually, I learned to type 60 words per minute.

The first day at this new school, my American History teacher asked me to stand up and introduce myself to the class because I was a new student. Then she said, "Today we will learn about the state capitals. Kim, since you came from California, do you know what the capital of California is?"

I was trembling. *Honestly,* I thought, *we lived in a tent in Camp Pendleton for a couple of months while waiting for a sponsor. I never had a chance to travel anywhere else in California nor learn anything about it.* The class was still in silence as they waited for my response. All of a sudden, I blurted, "Sacramento."

The teacher smiled, nodded her head, and clapped her hands. The entire class also clapped. I don't know why, but something inside my brain told me, *"It's not Los Angeles or San Francisco. It must be Sacramento."* These were the only cities in California I could remember. I sat down and breathed a sigh of relief.

One time, my history teacher made the class memorize the Gettysburg Address. I brought the homework home and put it in front of the kitchen sink on the counter trying to memorize while I was washing a big load of dishes. The paper became smeared and the ink smudged with water and detergent from the sink. Surprisingly, I did well and even received a perfect score on that quiz. My teacher told me after class that she was so proud of me and even gave me a small gift.

Our math teachers enrolled us in "Number Sense" and various other math contests for algebra and geometry. Participating in these events boosted my confidence level and opened a new horizon in teamwork and friendship. We also had a good coach, Ms. Y., who would comfort and encourage us even if we did not win. In one tournament, I cried tears of joy when I won a trophy in geometry; the first time I ever won anything in my life. I came home that day and excitedly showed my mom this small trophy. She said, "Good…Now go back to washing the dishes."

Every Sunday, we attended services, and the younger ones went to Sunday school at St. Mark's Episcopal Church. In Vietnam, Catholic churches and Buddhist temples are prevalent, so there was a refreshing novelty in the services at St. Mark's. My father continued his work there as a janitor.

The whole family especially enjoyed that Christmas season — our first Christmas in America. It is almost impossible to describe the mixed feelings of nostalgia each of us felt that day. We all went to church that Christmas Eve and had so much fun decorating the Christmas tree. I believe most, if not all, religion teaches goodness and tolerance, so it does not matter whether a person is an Episcopalian or a Buddhist, or maybe both. What matters is how we conduct our lives and what we bring to others that count.

I also remember going to work for the first time in America to earn money for a course in summer school. I didn't know that when you have a job you have to bring lunch money to purchase something to eat or bring a sack lunch. Having eaten only a banana for breakfast, I ended up starving at work from 7:30 in the morning until 5:30 that evening. I came home hungry and exhausted around 6:00 p.m. The two packages of noodles my mother prepared for me tasted better than any other food in my life at that time.

My brothers and sisters definitely experienced a learning curve in America. Television commercials bewildered us; some offered "free" items just by calling the number on the screen (which was also toll-free). Since my mom did not understand English, the children would call and ask for the "free" items. Soon enough, our house was filled with all kinds of brochures and booklets selling everything from gifts and gadgets to life insurance.

I continued to work and attend high school, and realized by keeping busy, that time would seem to fly by, and soon I could look forward to a new dream of attending college. Before I knew it, 1975 turned into 1976, and 1977 appeared to be reeling by at the same breakneck speed. Then, in the summer of 1977, my mother made an announcement that shook the foundations I had worked so hard to build in Texas.

CHAPTER 4

CALIFORNIA — HERE WE COME

It was July of 1977 when my mother told us we would be moving to Southern California. She briefly explained that there are more Vietnamese grocery stores, and the winter is milder there. We all stared at her in shock before we began asking excited questions. We did not have money to all fly on an airplane, so we would travel by bus instead.

The bus trip from Texas to California took a few days. Along the way, we enjoyed looking out the window and seeing long grassland prairies, plains, and different types of trees spotted across the horizon. We were amazed to see deserts and cactus for the first time as well. All eleven children behaved quite well on the bus, and some passengers even commended my mom on this fact. It was quite an exhausting but interesting trip.

Upon arrival in Southern California, we were supposed to stay temporarily at my mom's friend's house until we found a permanent place to settle. Little did we know, bad news was just around the corner. As we departed the bus and waited for my mom's friend, someone stole my father's briefcase that contained many of our important papers and documents. I remember my parents were so sad and upset because it would take a long time to apply and replace those documents.

We stayed at my mom's friend's house for several weeks while waiting for the paperwork and the documents. The family was hospitable, and my sisters and I quickly became friends with their children because of the proximity in our ages. We had so much fun just talking, laughing, and sharing stories. When I think back on these moments, I still remember the warmth and joy.

We moved to our own house in Buena Park. The woman across the street, Mrs. G., peeked in the window and saw that all of us slept on the floor with no bedding or furniture. She actually contacted a news television program and helped us get furniture and bedding through donations. It was a beautiful gesture by a good neighbor. Years later, I learned she had cancer and passed away. She is greatly missed.

I spent my junior and senior year at Cypress High School in Cypress, California. Every day, I attended class, and then worked after school in the school's library before going home in the evening. I did not make much money, but I gave my mom all that I earned to help with the family budget. At that time, there were no automatic scanners or computerized equipment. It was my job as a librarian assistant to shelf, stack books, and cross out the name of the borrowers, mostly students, on the library card. One day, I saw a strange name written on the library card of a book, "F...You", and I was not sure if it was a name or not. In my mind, I wondered if the last name of a person could be a pronoun. I brought it to the librarian and showed her, but she hastily told me to cross it out without even explaining why. It was not until I started college that I learned what those two words meant.

After my junior year, I got a partial scholarship to attend the Junior Statesmen of America Summer Session at the University of California in Davis (UC Davis). To make this possible financially, Cypress High School allowed me to work for a short time in the administration office and paid the remaining tuition. I got a chance to know the principal and the staff.

The Summer Session at UC Davis proved a fun and life-changing experience for me. It was my first time away from home, but the excitement of staying in a dorm, meeting new students, and learning about public speaking and government soon reduced my homesickness. UC Davis has a beautiful campus, and there I met many people who influenced me, including the professors, staff, and even politicians at the state capitol. Most importantly, I now had a taste of college life, and I liked it.

That summer was one of the best ones of my life. I actually met someone who I believed genuinely cared for me, who had a good character, and a good sense of humor. He could comfort me and make me laugh even on a "down" day. My English was not that good, but I remembered writing poems for him and receiving poems from him. At that time, I thought I might have a "crush" on him platonically, but he was never my boyfriend, and I was not interested yet in a physical relationship of any type. We remained friends for several years after that, and he helped me tremendously during my college years at Brown University. He brought me extra winter clothes and even helped with school essentials such as papers, a desk lamp, and an alarm clock while I was at Brown. More than thirty years later, thinking of that cherished summer and my first romantic friendship reminds me that our treasured moments can never be taken away, just as the love between a mother and her children is forever, despite the looming specter of autism.

During my senior year, I also took some night classes at Cypress College. Like many of my high school teachers, my college instructors were encouraging and supportive. In fact, I was surprised and grateful that one of my college instructors attended my high school graduation, since I was all alone that day. At that time, my father had just started a job as an electronic technician, a career that he earned by studying and training long hours. He was working extremely hard to support us; thus, I did not want to bother him with my graduation ceremony. My mom had to stay home and care for my younger siblings.

I was so proud to graduate with honors, even if I had to fight for it. My senior year had been busy, hectic, and exhausting, but I actually enjoyed it. At the end of the year, even though I had a high grade point average, the counselor did not enter my name for academic honors. She told me that the high schools I attended in Texas my first two years were not "academically acceptable."

The principal, Mr. B., came to my defense, however. He talked to her, and eventually she changed her mind. He told me he didn't care what school I had attended previously. "As long as when you came to my school you demonstrate that you could do the work, get A's, and maintain good citizenship, that's good enough for me," he said. He also told me that I should not be penalized just because my parents moved from Texas to California while I was in the middle of my high school years. I remembered receiving an award off-campus, and no one except my principal would take me there to receive it. I will never forget his kindness.

Although I was hopeful, deep down I still felt insecure and believed that no college would want me. I was screaming for joy when Brown University in Rhode Island sent me a letter of acceptance, with full scholarship. So, it was during April of 1979, that I had the difficult choice between Brown and the University of California in Berkeley (UC Berkeley). Had I gone to UC Berkeley, I would not have met my ex-husband, and perhaps, I would not be in the situation that I am in right now. I remember UC Berkeley asking me to turn in my acceptance card with a $50 deposit. I did not have the $50 deposit, so I chose Brown. Later on, I realized that the airplane ticket costs more than $50. Oh, well!

I became a member of Brown University's Class of 1983. Some people asked me why I applied to Brown. I told them, "I have never seen snow in my life." Years later, after living in Rhode Island, Vermont, and upstate New York, I rephrased that with, "I have never seen so much snow in my life."

Actually, the fact that the school name was a color and easy to pronounce played a major role in my decision-making process. At that time, if there were a college named Blue, I would have applied to that, too, although I am thinking now that I have a propensity for that name — after all, out of the entire doctors section of the Yellow Pages in San Antonio, I picked Dr. Brown.

While in college, I told myself I would not have a boyfriend because it would interfere with my studies. In fact, I would make myself ugly so no one would want me. That didn't work, though. After a couple of months at Brown, I actually had a boyfriend who later became my husband. I believe this was my destiny.

I graduated high school never having had a boyfriend, never been to a movie theater or seen a movie, never attended a teenage party, nor gone to a school dance or senior prom, smoked, drank, used a swear word, wore makeup, nor possessed or wore any jewelry. Until I turned eighteen years old, I thought that when you go to a movie theater, you actually get to see live actors perform there. Some students in high school swore at me, and I politely said, "Thank you very much." At that time, I did not understand what they said, but my teachers taught me to be polite and always say, "Thank you." When I turned eighteen and went off to college, I still had a lot to learn, but it wasn't just academics.

CHAPTER 5

BROWN UNIVERSITY – SWEET MEMORIES

When I told my supervisor at work, the Cypress High School librarian, that I'd been accepted to Brown, she told me I would be attending school with John F. Kennedy, Jr. I vaguely remembered reading about his father in my history and government classes. I had never seen a picture of John, Jr., and I quickly forgot about what she said. After all, I was just a poor, little girl working hard to get a good education so I could one day help my family.

That summer before arriving at Brown, I worked extra hours to earn as much money as possible. As the second oldest daughter in a family of 11 children, I wanted to alleviate some of the financial burden my parents faced every day. Ever since I came to California and started working daily after school, I never once thought of keeping any money for myself. When I purchased my airline ticket to get to Brown, it represented the first time I had to spend some of my working money on myself. After saving enough money for an airplane ticket and the bus fare to Providence, I gave the remaining money to my mom.

A week before the actual flight, I started to pack and noticed that all my clothes were either worn-out, faded, or had holes in them. I asked my mom to drop me off at a local Good Will or Pic-N-Save store to buy some clothes. I remembered picking out quite a few "comfortable" clothes, not knowing that those were maternity pants and dresses. I didn't understand why some of the students at Brown looked at my stomach whenever I wore those dresses. One of them asked me how far along I was. I replied, "My dorm is not very far at all."

I needed a heavy coat and boots to prepare for the winter weather in Rhode Island, but this particular store did not have them. They pointed me to another store where the price was exorbitant. I told myself that I could always search for Good Will stores around Brown; the East Coast stores might carry heavy winter clothing.

The trip from the West Coast to the East Coast constituted my first time ever traveling alone by airplane. I did not like flying at all, and I felt nauseated during the airplane take-off and landing. I also felt a bit nervous about getting on an airplane and prayed during most of the flight. When the plane landed safely at Boston's Logan Airport, I was overjoyed. My joy turned into worry quickly when I realized I had barely enough money to pay for the bus to Providence. In fact, I did not have any money left to pay for the taxi from the Providence bus station to Brown University. The taxi driver had to stop at a payphone in front of Brown so I could call the orientation coordinator. She came out and paid for the $2.78 taxi fare. When winter came, the school also gave me some money to buy winter clothes.

While at Brown, I was enrolled in the Work-Study Program to make extra money for books and other expenses. I remembered working in the cafeteria my first semester, the dean's office my second semester, and the Engineering Department thereafter. My supervisor in the cafeteria was a friendly and polite upperclassman from Maine majoring in international relations. The first few days I didn't know what to do and was clumsy. He patiently taught me. I accidentally spilled the salad dressing on his shoes, dropped a couple of plates, and broke a glass, but he did not get angry with me and even helped me clean up. I naively asked him while he tried to pick up the broken pieces of glass, "Sorry…I'll be more careful. Are you upset at me?" He shook his head and smiled, "No…because I like you." He also helped me carrying heavy containers since I was a small 5-foot-2-inch slender girl of just 88 pounds. After the shift was over, he gave me an apple and an orange to take back to the dorm. He seemed to care for me, and he treated me with respect and kindness.

While working with Dean A. and his secretary, who were always kind, professional, and never condescending, I was privileged to see visitors who came to campus. One afternoon, a pretty young lady showed up and asked for directions to her brother's dorm. I didn't know who she was at first, but the secretary introduced us, and I learned that she was Caroline Kennedy. I told Caroline that I happened to share the same dorm as her brother John and would be happy to tell her how to get there. Thinking back to that moment, I was amazed at how graceful and soft-spoken she was.

Several months later, one of the Engineering professors allowed me to work in the same lab with his graduate students. I vividly recall my first meeting with Professor T. I wanted to do undergraduate work in a lab, but I did not know how to apply for this honor. It was after dinner one day that I came by the B&H Engineering building to pick up some graded homework. At the time, there were no laptops, cell phones, or e-mail, and although I could make an appointment through the secretary, it was just as quick and easy to call directly or stop by professors' offices.

All of the professors I wanted to see had left for the day because it was already past dinner time. I looked underneath the door of one professor's office and his office light was still on. I had never met him previously or taken a course with him, and he did not know me. I also did not have my resume with me when I hesitantly knocked on his door. He opened the door and seemed surprised to see me. "Do we have an appointment? Do I know you?" He asked.

I nervously looked at him; my heart felt like it was about to jump out of my chest. I took a deep breath and immediately introduced myself. After warming up and gathering all my courage, I asked if I could have a job working in his lab.

I assumed all the professors had labs with graduate students conducting research projects. He was reluctant at first but then told me to wait for him in his office. I thought he was checking the secretary book or the department finance record to see if there was a budget to hire one more student. About ten minutes later, he returned and told me, "Here is the situation. I have three graduate students working in my lab. I asked them. One of them said 'no'; two of them said 'yes'..." He paused. I thought I would not get a chance to work in his lab. Then he continued, "But in America, majority rules! So it's okay...you can start tomorrow."

I had quite a learning curve, but I enjoyed working in Professor T.'s lab as well as working in Professor S.' lab the following year.

During my undergraduate years at Brown, many times I worked over thirty-five hours in one week. Each payday, I sent money orders home. Even though my grades were not perfect, I was proud of the effort and the contribution I made to help my family. One of my professors voiced his concern about my load and wanted me to cut down on my work hours; he even asked me, "Do you come to Brown to study or to work?"

One of my engineering professors, Professor K., taught me Electrical & Mechanical Systems. He was tall, gray-haired, and had a hoarse voice. When I went to see him during office hours, as he drew the circuits to help me with my homework, I noticed he had several blotches on his skin, but I attributed them to old age. Sometimes he seemed tired and his voice became hoarser than usual, but he never wanted to stop until I understood the concepts.

I remember our last meeting as if I was still standing in his doorway. I had completed all my degree requirements one semester early and was about to move to Vermont to work for IBM. I stopped by his office to say goodbye. We chatted quite a bit that day, and as I walked out the door he asked, "Kim, will you come back to visit me someday?"

I replied, "Don't worry. When I become rich and famous I will come back to visit you."

He laughed, "And how are you supposed to do that?" He always asked me that question after drawing out the circuit diagram. However, this time, there was no circuit diagram, and he caught me off-guard. I did not know what to say, and without thinking I blurted out, "Win the lottery..." We both laughed so hard. We shared the last innocent, silly, and genuine laugh between a humble student and a dedicated professor.

As the years went by, I was busy with my life and family and regret I never got a chance to go back and see him. Years later, I read in the Brown Alumni Magazine that he passed away. The article mentioned that he had terminal skin cancer but decided to spend his remaining years teaching and being with his students. I did not want to cry in front of my husband and children, but the tears of sadness and guilt slowly rolled down my face. I still regret not letting him know how much I appreciated him: not even a postcard, a letter, or a box of chocolates. As a promise to him, I vowed at that moment that as soon as I finished any other course I would come back and give each teacher, instructor, or professor a small token of appreciation.

I have never become rich and famous and never won the lottery, but he and Professor T. enriched my life and helped me succeed in so many ways. Overall, my experience at Brown University gave me the strength and courage to overcome many challenges later in life.

It was a few weeks before Christmas in 1979, and I already had sent my last paycheck money order home. I had no money left for an airplane ticket. Walking down Thayer Street in Providence one afternoon, I was feeling sad and lonely. I missed my parents and my brothers and sisters. Then a thought crossed my mind. I remembered someone told me I could buy things at the Brown bookstore and charge them to my account, which meant I could pay for them later in installments. I rushed to the bookstore, browsed the entire store to find gift items for all my family members, and asked to have them wrapped in Christmas wrapping paper. It took me about three hours but finally, I found myself leaving the bookstore holding two big bags of presents. Now I just had to ask a favor from one of my classmates who would be traveling back to California to visit his family — to take them back to my family with him.

As I walked toward my dorm with one large shopping bag in each hand, I heard a voice behind me, "Do you need some help?" I turned around and saw him. He was a tall young man with a head of bulky brown, wavy hair and a warm husky voice. I thought I might have seen him around campus, but I couldn't recall where, and I didn't think we'd been introduced before. He smiled, and I could tell by the way he smiled and the look in his eyes he was a genuinely nice person. I stopped so he could catch up with me, and I handed him one of my bags. His right hand barely touched my left hand as he took it from me. Even though it was a cool afternoon, my hand was cold; his was much warmer. "Oh, sorry...Thank you." I smiled shyly at him. I didn't know what else to say and apologized for touching him.

As we walked side by side, we began to talk. He made a brief comment about the weather, but I forgot exactly what he said. I barely looked at him because I was so shy. He asked where I was heading, and I said back to the dorm. That's when we discovered that we shared the same dorm, Littlefield, and he was heading that way, too.

Then I remembered. I had seen him in front of Littlefield the first week of school. I was up in my room on the second floor studying when I looked out the window and saw this boy doing a handstand near a tree. I was amused and amazed because I had never seen anyone doing the handstand. Before I could comment about his talent, he asked me about the bags. "They're presents for my parents and ten siblings," I explained. "I won't be going home for Christmas."

"Wow...big family..." he said with obvious surprise.

"How many brothers and sisters do you have?"

"One sister. Why aren't you going home for Christmas?"

I almost told him I had no money for the plane ticket, but instead I offered a secondary reason. "I'm afraid of flying. When the airplane takes off and lands, I pray I won't throw up and that there will not be a crash."

He burst into laughter, but then stopped and said, "You shouldn't be afraid of flying. Flying is fun." Then he said something about the safety statistics being much better for flying than for driving. As we continued to walk he told me about his love of flying and his desire to become a pilot someday. I told him I just wanted to have an ordinary family: a husband who loved and cared for me and maybe one or two children — definitely not eleven. I put the bag in front of me and walked as if I were pregnant, which made both of us laugh.

A sudden cool breeze sent shivers down my neck and spine as it blew my long black hair toward him. He quickly glanced at me and asked if I was cold. He even offered to let me use his jacket, but I repeatedly shook my head and said I was not cold. Then we talked about our majors. I told him mine was probably going to be engineering. He mentioned that his major was probably going to be political science.

"Your major is hard," he said.

"Yours is one thousand times more difficult," I replied. We laughed again. Then he asked about my hometown, and I said I was from California. He told me he came from New York. He asked me why I decided to come all the way to the East Coast for school. There were many reasons, but I just remember one major reason, so I said, "To see snow." We both laughed so hard this time we could hardly stop.

I can't explain why, but I felt his warmth and genuineness radiate toward me. Even though I had just met him and barely knew him, I felt like I had known him before. For the first time, I turned my head slightly toward him and looked closely. He also turned slightly toward me and looked at me. His eyes met mine. In those brief moments, time stood still. We stopped laughing and just looked at each other…in silence.

I never had an older brother, but I always wished I had one. At that moment, how I wish I had an older brother like him, someone to whom I could talk, with whom I could share a laugh, and with whom I could confide my secrets and worries—someone who could help relieve a heavy burden on my shoulders.

Suddenly we both became very quiet; we were approaching the door of Littlefield Hall. It is as if we recognized that all good things have to come to an end. He turned to me and said, "By the way, I am John and you are…"

41

"Kim," I said.

He opened the door for me and carried the bag all the way up-stairs to my room on the second floor. As soon as he handed the bag back to me in front of my dorm room, a few of the girls on that floor saw him and screamed, "John F. Kennedy, Jr., John F. Kennedy, Jr. carried the bag for you. Oh my God..." I barely was able to thank him through the noise of their screams; he turned red with embarrassment and ran quickly upstairs to his room. I felt sad. I had so enjoyed his company. I didn't know who he was before, but I wished he were another John.

Then I thought about how lucky I was to have met him and shared a good conversation with him. Somehow, he changed my perception of "rich and famous" people. I thought about how nice he was, and what a good upbringing his mother had given him — someone who was raised in power and privilege yet was still gra-cious and genuine. I thought about the son of a former president helping carry a bag for the daughter of a former janitor. *Well, that's the end of it,* I thought.

I didn't think much about our chance meeting that afternoon until chance brought us together again. I remember missing an En-gineering 3 class and wanting to borrow notes from a classmate, John M., on the fourth floor. I went upstairs and knocked on the door of his room, but he wasn't there. Suddenly, I heard a voice be-hind me saying, "Hi, can I help you?" I turned around and, surpris-ingly, it was John, Jr. Apparently he had just come out of the show-er. He was standing there with a white towel wrapped around his waist and water dripping off his hair. He smiled warmly at me and said, "John is my roommate. He's in the bathroom showering."

"I'll just wait for a few minutes in the hallway," I said softly. Perhaps John, Jr. didn't want me to wait alone in the hallway, so he hung around for a little while, and we talked mostly about school. Then he jokingly mentioned something that made me laugh so hard I almost cried. More than 30 years later, I still remember like it was yesterday the way he said it, so funny and so amazingly witty. Whenever I am having a down day, I always remember his joke, and it brings a smile to my face. I ended up leaving a note for John

M. and was about to leave when, surprisingly, John Jr. gave me a small gift.

Every now and then, I would see him in front of Littlefield, and he always said, "Hi, Kim," and opened the door for me, even when he was talking on the phone. If I had to choose two words to describe him, I would use "gracious" and "gallant."

About a week later, I was in the lounge studying, when W.C., a Littlefield dorm-mate and the boyfriend of one of the girls on my floor, came by to say he was organizing the Secret Santa gift exchange for Littlefield Hall. I needed to pick a Secret Santa by drawing a name randomly out of a container. After he shuffled the pieces, I closed my eyes, and with my left hand, I randomly picked out a tiny piece of paper. I opened it in front of him. The name read John F. Kennedy, Jr. He was surprised, and so was I. Then he told me the rule for the gift exchange involved giving the person you'd chosen a daily gift valued around $10 or less for a week prior to the actual Secret Santa party. The actual present could be anything nice.

I went out to dinner at the Ratty that evening with my then-boyfriend, who later became my husband, thinking of what I should give John, Jr. that he did not already have; especially because I did not have much money anyway. My boyfriend was a bit jealous when he noticed that I became preoccupied with the Secret Santa gift. Suddenly, I knew exactly what to give him, and I promised that it would be something special.

After coming back to my room, I was so embarrassed when a few girls loudly screamed in the hallway, "Kim got Kennedy…Kim got Kennedy." It was supposed to be a secret. That's why it was called Secret Santa. Who told them? Then I looked at one of the girls and recognized her as W.C.'s girlfriend.

Later that night, W.C. came by and told me I needed to pick another Secret Santa. He shuffled the tiny drawing papers again, and I reached in and randomly picked one. I opened it in front of him, and this time I had a different Secret Santa. W.C. was surprised again. In fact, my second Secret Santa's name also was John. This time it was John M., John F. Kennedy, Jr.'s roommate.

Every day of the week I put a present in front of his door, and all I wrote on it was "To John…From Your Secret Santa." It did not matter to me which John received it. Then on the day of the party when we all revealed our Secret Santa with a gift, I gave John M. a gift, but not the gift I had intended for John, Jr.

A thought crossed my mind. I intended to keep my commitment to my initial Secret Santa. A few days later, I completed my gift and left it in front of his room with no explanation about the Secret Santa's situation.

That evening John, Jr. found me and thanked me. He greeted me with that same warm smile. His face and his eyes lit up. "I really liked the gift, Kim. Where did you buy it?"

"I didn't. I made it."

"Wow," he said and smiled broadly. I noted the same level of surprise and amazement that I felt when I saw him doing the handstand under the tree in front of Littlefield. Then I tried to tell him about the Secret Santa's situation, but my English was probably not articulate enough for him to understand. It did not matter. I put everything behind me, and we each went on with our lives.

Over the years at Brown I met many nice and caring students at Brown. How grateful I was to get the packages of Campbell's Chicken Noodle Soup and Krispy Crackers from the resident counselor at Littlefield that Christmas recess since the cafeteria was closed. She must have known that I did not have enough money to buy food until it reopened after the recess. Meeting John, Jr., however, was one of my most poignant and sweetest memories at Brown. Second semester, I moved to a different dorm, and thereafter I stayed at the Graduate Center, where I was lucky to have a single room of my own. I didn't see him as often after that.

Years later, I was too busy with my daily challenges to watch TV, movies, or pay attention to the news. At night, sometimes I turned on the TV just to catch up a bit with current events. Every now and then, I heard about John F. Kennedy, Jr., on the news, but then I quickly put the story out of my mind, partly because I did not believe or agree with the pundits' comments about him or his family.

It was not until one early July morning in 1999 that my fond memories of him rekindled. My daughter woke up and wanted to watch cartoons on TV. The night before, my son was crying off and on, and I hardly managed even a few hours of sleep. I was a bit sleepy when I grabbed the remote control and inadvertently pushed the cable button to the CNN channel. The tragic events I saw unfolding on TV that morning forever imprints on my mind. At first, I thought I was having a bad dream. CNN reported that John F. Kennedy, Jr.'s plane disappeared from the radar during a night flight. Deep down inside I knew the chance was very, very slim, but I continued to hope and pray for him, his wife, and his sister-in-law.

Things did not turn out the way I wished. The plane wreckage and the bodies were found a few days later underneath the Atlantic Ocean. I cried a lot that day and over the next several days. Even though my own life was a wreck, I was happy for him when he founded *George* magazine and later found true love in Carolyn Bessette. I thought about the conversation that we had on the way to Littlefield and his love of flying. I thought about how each of us was pursuing a different dream; his dream was cut short, and mine did not come true. I thought about the girl who was mesmerized by the boy doing the handstand. I thought about the gift I gave him, and the gift that he gave me. I have never revealed that gift to anyone, and I will let it be buried in the same ocean and in the sands of time. I bid a fond farewell to John, Jr., the prince of Camelot, the kindest and nicest royal person I have ever known.

The timing of these tragic events tied themselves so coincidentally to the demise of my own dreams, my own family, that only the knowledge that there are people out there who *are* genuine and kind, can pull us above the abyss of our emotions. I would rely on that heavily from now on.

CHAPTER 6

MY MARRIAGE AND MY EX-HUSBAND

It takes two people to create a marriage or to dissolve one. I was a young, innocent, and naïve eighteen year old when I met my husband, and in retrospect, I had many could haves, would haves, and should haves. While we shared a few cultural and traditional values in common, we were two different individuals with different interests and goals. It would be just as simple to say we had "irreconcilable differences," but life is never that simple. We did not have a crystal ball to help us fathom the immense stress — physically, psychologically, and financially — of raising three children with autism. Perhaps the stress was just too much for both of us. Perhaps he did love his children, but he loved his other interests more — or maybe those interests helped him forget about the stress at home and the problems his children brought to our lives.

In hindsight, I believe our relationship was doomed from the very beginning — with or without the children — and we both made the mistake of trying to change each other, trying to hold on to something that wasn't there. I also believe he was not ready to be a father at that time, or at least, he was not the "father type." In addition, when you have children with any type of disability or medical conditions, it requires tremendous commitment and compromise to make a lasting relationship.

Divorce was the best thing for both of us. I finally found the internal peace and happiness that had eluded me all my life. He finally had the freedom to pursue his interests and dreams. It took me a long time, but I am finally able to let go of the bitterness and the pain in our 15 years of marriage. I harbor no hard feelings or bitterness toward him, and I wish him well. He has always honored our visitation arrangements as well as his financial obligations. Someone once told me that the best way to heal and become whole again is to tell your story and hope it helps and heals others.

It was around the first week of October 1979 when I met him at Brown. On a windy afternoon, he accidentally bumped into me in front of the library and caused my books and papers to scatter on the ground.

"I'm sorry." He apologized and helped me picked them up.

"That's OK. Don't worry about it." I replied softly. I barely looked at him as both of us chasing after the papers flying in all directions. Finally, we got all the papers. I was about to say thank you and walk away, when suddenly, he looked closely at me and asked me if I was Vietnamese, which I nodded. Then he switched to the Vietnamese greeting and asked me my name. I was caught off-guard since he was the first Vietnamese guy that I met, and I didn't know how to address him in Vietnamese. I recalled when there is a man coming over to my house, usually my parent's friend, my mom always tell me to greet him, "Da, chao Chu" or "Da, chao Bac," a greeting title for someone who is much older than I am.

"Da, chao Chu." I greeted him. He was surprised that I called him "Chu," and I could tell he was upset. "You know that I'm not that old," he said in Vietnamese.

"Oh, sorry…Da, chao Bac." I said with a trembling voice. "Bac" is another saluting term for someone who is fairly old, even older than the first greeting term. He busted into laughter and told me that he might have seen me around the school, and once again asked me my name. I composed myself and told him my name. He later said that I could just call him by "Anh."

I had never met him before, but my first impression of him was not terrific. *He's ugly and has a loud voice*, I thought. I've always told

47

myself that appearance makes little difference to me; the inside of the person is much more important. Furthermore, I've always thought of myself as an "ugly duckling" anyway. I was a bit reserved with him at first, but he seemed open. We stood and talked for a while in the midst of a windy afternoon. I found out that he was a graduate student in chemistry and he came from a poor family just like mine, but he seemed smart and worked hard like me.

At that time, I was having trouble with my chemistry class, and he offered to help. I love to eat Vietnamese and Chinese food, and he offered to take me out to eat. One thing led to another; I became his girlfriend. One of my engineering classmates saw the two of us walking together, and he would later tell me in class in the nicest way possible, "Kim, your boyfriend is 'handsome opposite'." I had never dated before, and he definitely taught me more than chemistry. I had never had a boyfriend, but he had several girlfriends before me.

Years later, he told me that it was my innocence and naiveté that caught his attention. Perhaps I was lonely and wanted to have a friend, an older brother figure that I can talk and relate to. I'd never wanted a relationship, but it happened. It wasn't long before I discovered that I felt uncomfortable in a relationship. I felt that being with him took too much time away from studying, but I was afraid to say so for fear of hurting his feelings. As time went on, it became clear we had little in common besides a love of Vietnamese food. In fact, we didn't even like the same kind of music. However, sometimes one cannot escape the wide net of destiny.

In the summer of 1981, I was thrilled to have a job at IBM in Essex Junction, Vermont. Although my time there went by quickly, I was glad to have met several students from other colleges (Cornell, MIT, RPI, and University of Illinois at Urbana-Champaign) around the country who also worked at IBM that summer. My boyfriend came to visit me, submitted an application to IBM for full-time work, and was hired. After completing my degree at the beginning of 1983, I also got a job offer there; thus, we both ended up with jobs at IBM and at the same location.

We bought a small house in Vermont. I continued to pursue my graduate study in electrical engineering at the University of Vermont (UVM) by taking courses in the evening and at night while working during the day. The professors at UVM were very helpful and understanding.

I was fortunate to work at IBM, an excellent company, for over twelve years, but I was more fortunate to meet and work with so many bright, friendly, and talented individuals. It was such an enjoyable and fascinating experience working with them. While I loved working for IBM in general and did so at other locations as well, my time at IBM in Essex Junction, Vermont was among the best in my professional career thus far.

After my graduation from the University of Vermont in 1986, we planned to get married. To do so, both of us had to go through a blood test screening first as required by the state of Vermont. Shortly after that, we received a letter in the mail indicating that we both needed to have rubella vaccinations. The place where we went for our rubella vaccination was a small health office or a small clinic that resembled a military office. We arrived late in the afternoon, and we were the only ones there; however, we waited what seemed an eternity before we received our shots. I did not think much about it, except, *let's get this over and done with.*

He had hoped to change me, perhaps into a more traditional, docile, and "absolute obedient" wife; I hoped to change him, perhaps to a more caring and "family-oriented" husband as part of an equal team. I met him in 1979, and we got married in 1987. Someone once told me: "It's not how long you've known someone; it's how well you know them." To this day, I don't think I really "knew" him well. At that time, I felt we had been with each other for a long time. Since I was already intimate with him, I didn't want to leave him and hoped that with marriage and children, he would change. Unfortunately, dreams do not always become a reality. Years later, I realized he never did change. I was alone then, and I remained alone.

CHAPTER 7

MY SON – THE HAPPINESS

AND THE HEARTACHE

During the year of 1987 through 1988, IBM assigned both my husband and me to jobs in California. While there, I learned I was pregnant with my son. Although we did not plan to have a child so soon after our marriage, the pregnancy came as a happy surprise for both of us. But like everything else in my life, the happiness was short-lived. We moved back to Vermont when I was six months pregnant. Except for one UTI and one mild food poisoning incident, it was a smooth pregnancy.

After a long, arduous, and exhaustive labor, my son, Nam, was born via a normal delivery in 1988. I cried tears of joy to see my precious bundle: a 9 pound, 3 ounce, healthy and beautiful baby boy. The first few months were amazing. I never got over the fact that he was so sweet and so lovely; he even slept through the night within a few months. My sister-in-law from Connecticut came to help for a week after my son's birth. In fact, she also came to help with both of my daughters' arrivals, and my husband and I stayed at their place for a short time while moving from Burlington, Vermont, to upstate New York. Regardless of my feelings for my ex-husband, my sister-in-law, my brother-in-law, and my two nephews have been very kind to me and the children over the years. My sister-in-law was an amazing and gracious woman who passed away suddenly in 2010. Her kindness and graciousness will be long-remembered, appreciated, and greatly missed.

After the birth of my son, I stayed home for several months before heading back to work in the evenings. My husband cared for Nam in the evening while I took care of him in the morning until around 3:00 p.m. We wrote down all his feedings, naps and activities in a small notebook. He usually napped when I started to leave the house, and he seemed to have a reasonable appetite when he woke up.

In retrospect, I wish I had stayed home instead of going back to work, and that I had breastfed him a bit longer rather than bottle-feeding him. Both Nam's younger sisters, Lan and Mai, were breastfed until they turned one year old. I do not know if that would have made any difference, but I still harbor a feeling of guilt somewhere in my conscience.

I loved Nam so much. I spent as much time with him as I could. We watched television shows (*Sesame Street and Mickey Mouse*), played toys, and watched music videos together. I also brought him to see other kids in the neighborhood; he was not interested in playing with them. I thought he was a bit shy. He was slow in his developmental milestones. Other people would tell me that the first-born child sometimes tends to be slow. Yet, I sensed something was wrong. He played with toys inappropriately (rolling the wheels of a car, twirling, chewing, squeezing), and he did not want to cuddle much. Nam also fixated on certain things (hand gestures, a certain colored toy, toothpaste), rocked a lot, and repeatedly vocalized some unintelligible sounds. Sometimes it seemed as if he was in his own world and did not even turn around when I called him, yet his hearing test was normal. When he was between one and two years old, he began to cry sometimes for no apparent reason. I also noticed he had a high pain tolerance threshold.

I reluctantly went back to work in the first shift when he was around two and a half years old and brought him to a babysitter's house. The babysitter had several small children, and I was hoping that as they played together, he would gain more communication and social skills. There were times I had to come and pick him up early, however, because the babysitter called me at work and told me that he cried constantly for no apparent reason (no fall, no fever, and no hunger). She also noticed that he did not want to play with the other kids. I thought it was because of separation anxiety, so I came during my lunch hour to see him and feed him. This did not help.

Nam's receptive and expressive language skills were definitely behind other kids around his age. He was able to say about 20 words (car, mama, daddy, eat, drink, sleep, house, airplane) and a few very short phrases (I cry, where is mommy, mommy right here, take a bath, my blanket) when he was close to two years old. However, by the time he reached four years old he seemed to lose most, if not all, the language or communication skills he had acquired to that point and replaced these with more crying off and on.

I brought him to the pediatrician many times. At first, the pediatrician, Dr. B., took the "wait and see" approach, but eventually he did recommend that we see the Vermont Child Development Clinic staff for evaluation. Upon initial evaluation, they noted, "Nam is exhibiting a global development delay with significant decreased communication skills and social skills." They also recommended bringing Nam to the Center for Disorders of Communication for evaluation in speech/language/hearing, starting Nam in Essential Early Education (EEE), and having a blood test for lead poisoning. The lead test came back negative.

We brought Nam to see one specialist after another. Our trip took us from the East Coast to the West Coast to see many specialists for assessments and consultations including the UCLA Center for Child Development.

All the specialists came to the same diagnosis: severe autism, an incurable neurological disease that impairs social interaction, communication, and behavioral skills. Some also diagnosed him with autism and mental retardation. It was the first time I had ever heard of autism, and I didn't even know what it meant. The more I read about it, the more questions I had, although most of my questions began with "Why?" I felt like I was completely in the dark, fumbling to shed light on the disease for myself so I could understand it and why my child had it. This was not easy given that there was not a lot of literature about autism at that time.

The day I received Nam's diagnosis was one of the saddest days of my life, a nightmare from which I could not wake up or walk away. I thought about the challenges ahead, and I remembered crying myself to sleep that night. Nam was about three and a half years old when he was diagnosed with autism. The road ahead for us would be long and steep.

Programs for autistic children at the time were limited, so we tried to enhance his communication and social skills with small playgroup activities and enrolled him in the EEE special program at a preschool. It was quite a task to teach him anything at all. If he was not constantly moving, then he would be crying and banging his head or doing other self-stimulating behaviors, such as chewing on random things, gesturing strangely with his hands, sucking his thumb, poking at his hand or fingers, rocked repeatedly on the chair, etc. We tried different methods to reduce his "stimming" behaviors but none seemed to work. We also thought about his future; he needed a sibling to care for him if something happened to us. At times, I hugged him tightly, but I felt that he was withering and slipping away, and there was little I could do to prevent this from happening. In the pit of my being, I felt heaviness and sadness, all of it exacerbated by the foreboding sense that I was going to be alone.

One day, my husband and I came to Dr. K., the Vermont Child Development Clinic Developmental pediatrician, to discuss the possibility of having another child. He gave my son a blood test called Fragile X syndrome. Since the result was negative, he told us it would be okay to have more children. In hindsight, I wish he had advised us differently. However, I don't blame him, and I don't have time to focus on what might have been. I believe Dr. K. did the best he could, given the limited data that was available to him at the time.

In 1992, when Nam was about four years old, we moved from Vermont to New York as my husband started on a new project that required relocation. We settled in Hopewell Junction, New York, and Nam attended Children's Annex, a special day program for children with autism. At this time, there was clear evidence that his communication abilities, especially his expressive and receptive language abilities, had diminished almost completely and been replaced with more crying episodes accompanied with head banging. Every time he started doing this, I would have to put pillows around him to prevent him from hurting his head. Sometimes he experienced bloody noses because of his intense crying episodes.

I had a candid discussion with the principal of Children's Annex, and I asked her if my son would ever talk again. She told me that in all her years working with autistic children, it seemed the percentage of children who acquired verbal skills and lost them, and later regained them was low; however, the percentage of children who never had verbal ability and later improved in verbal skills, language, and communication was quite high. Years later, I recalled this conversation, and her statement resonated with me. My oldest son never regained his verbal communication; my younger daughter would fall into the latter category.

Despite the odds and statistics, I continued to work on improving my son's verbal skills by engaging him with talking toys, flashcards, and audiovisual activities. Every day, a county school bus came to pick up my son from Hopewell Junction to bring him to Children's Annex in Kingston, which was about two hours away from my house. On heavy snow days, sometimes the bus didn't bring him home until around 6:00 p.m. I kept on looking out the window waiting for his bus and was worried sick. During this time, I became pregnant with our second child, and I thought about leaving work permanently to stay home and take care of my children. I still felt guilty about going back to work so soon after my son was born.

The weather was cold, windy, and snowy every winter in upstate New York. I had come to realize how lonely and vulnerable I felt and how I needed a shoulder to cry on. The heat was on in my home, but I felt like there was a draft and a snow drift within the walls of the house; it seemed much colder inside than outside. My husband did not seem capable of giving me the love, warmth, and comfort I needed. I don't know if Nam's condition caused us to drift farther apart or simply the stress of trying to work and deal with parenting, but our differences were becoming more and more apparent. I took some time off from work to care for my son and prepare for the arrival of my daughter. Nam was sick quite often. One time we took Nam to the pediatrician, Dr. C., who told us he had pneumonia and needed to have a chest X-ray. During the procedure, he cried hard, but I could not come in and comfort him because I was six months pregnant. With intensive treatment, he eventually recovered from his pneumonia.

My second pregnancy was uneventful, except for a number of tests I had done, such as a glucose tolerance test and amniocentesis. My husband demanded that I abort if the amniocentesis result came back positive for any abnormalities. The result was negative — the best Christmas present I could have received that year.

It was in the morning near the end of March 1993 when I began to feel the contractions. My husband told me he was in a meeting that day, so I tried not to call him until around noon. He brought some food home, but I could hardly eat anything because the contractions became more regular, intense, and painful. Finally, I told him to bring me to the doctor. I was so surprised when the doctor told me I was 9 centimeters dilated already. My husband had to rush home to pick up my son. At first, the nurse was planning to call 911 to get an ambulance to take me to the hospital, but my kind and caring obstetrician, Dr. Z., offered to drive me to the hospital in Poughkeepsie, which was about 40 minutes away. The nurse accompanied him, brought along a bucket with blanket, towel, scissors and other emergency packages. I knew the gravity of the situation — I could have given birth anytime, a roadside delivery.

Along the way, Dr. Z. flagged down a police car which guided us to the hospital and helped us pass several red lights. He also held my hand and comforted me the whole time as the nurse helped me through every contraction. After the hospital staff checked me into the room, Dr. P., the doctor on duty at the hospital that day, delivered my daughter. We named her Lan, the name for a Vietnamese orchid. When I first held her and looked at her, I knew she had my husband's face. Over the years, as my children grew up, they all resembled my husband. Some people would say, "Lan looks identical to your husband!" And they were right: the loud voice, posture, face, and even the extreme under bite.

The delivery happened so quickly that my husband barely made it in time. I also missed Nam terribly and asked him to bring our son in for a quick visit. I was so glad to see Nam and was thrilled that he did not have a crying episode while in the hospital. I told him to come closer so I could hug him, but he just stood there. He stood in a corner near the hospital bed, staring at me for a while, and suddenly said "Mom" in Vietnamese "*Me.*" I was so touched that I cried. Although he seemed to stop talking completely at five years old, he still remembered that I was his mom. This would be his very last word ever to me. How I wished I had a recorder to tape him as he said it.

At five years of age, Nam just seemed lost in so many ways. He cried constantly, banged his head, rocked back and forth, and had bloody noses so often. For a brief period, we tried giving him Tylenol, but the result was inconsistent. We had been told that it might help calm him down. Sometimes it helped; sometimes he continued to cry until he was exhausted and fell asleep. He also played with toys inappropriately and seemed to be in his own world quite often. I knew he was autistic because of what the professionals had told me, but deep down inside I was holding on to a tiny dream that a miracle might happen and that someday he would talk and be normal.

At that time (1993-1996) the pediatric neurologist in New York, Dr. W., had tried different medications for Nam such as Ritalin, Inderal, B6, and Tegretol, but none seemed to help. He even recommended an EEG and MRI of the brain for Nam in 1993. The EEG was normal and so was the brain MRI. As his crying episodes intensified so did the nosebleeds. Nam had one nasal cauterization with general anesthesia the same year. We took him to most of the recommended professionals and even tried to see a few of the well-known pioneers in autism. We tried everything for him including social groups, imitation, medication, mega-vitamins, special diets, behavior modification, facilitators, and even nontraditional eastern medicine. Nothing seemed to improve his communication ability, social deficits or reduce his crying episodes. I had desperate moments when I thought about giving him a part of my brain if that would help him recover.

But now I had another child to consider and care for as well. I had to put some of my attention on Lan as well. So, I split my focus to the best of my ability.

CHAPTER 8

MY MIDDLE CHILD – A DAUGHTER

WHO BRINGS HOPE

I channeled most of my remaining energy into monitoring my newborn daughter for signs and symptoms of autism. My daughter was born a healthy girl at 8 pounds, 8 ounces. She was breastfed along with bottle supplements. She seemed bright and was lovely to look at. All her developmental milestones were within normal limits; if anything, they were on the fast track. She could talk when she was around a year old and recited the alphabet at around 18 months old. Compared to my son, she did not appear to have any major delays in cognitive, communication, and social development within the first two years. She was a bit shy, usually looking down or elsewhere when I talked to her. Many times, she also repeated words or phrases just spoken by me or my husband in a conversation. However, I focused more upon her cognitive abilities and communication skills. Maybe I was so relieved that she did not have the same signs and symptoms that her brother had at her age that I overlooked some other autistic features that she did demonstrate, such as poor eye contact and echolalia, the automatic repetition of vocalizations made by another person.

As a toddler, Lan loved to watch TV shows such as *Barney* and *Sesame Street* as well as other shows on PBS and Disney, and movies like *Winnie the Pooh*. I was so thrilled with her cognitive development and academic ability. She also enjoyed watching music videos, such as *Kidsongs* and *Barney Songs*. She could not interact with her brother much because of his frequent crying episodes and his lack of verbal and nonverbal communication. Although she did not seem to be bothered by Nam's crying, I usually brought her to another room when Nam started to cry and bang his head. Because she could talk, my husband spent a little more time with her than her brother. I remember Lan repeatedly asked for Eeyore, a character in the *Winnie the Pooh* video, and we visited many stores before we could find the Eeyore stuffed animal for her. Whenever we got the chance, we took her to the mall, park, restaurant, and other places in the neighborhood so she could interact with other children.

At that time, I had no reason to believe that Lan would be autistic. Many of her fears, fixations, resistance to change, and repetitive behaviors seemed to develop later. I was approaching my mid-thirties, and I could feel my biological clock starting to tick. I thought about having one more child so my daughter could have a brother or sister to play with, and hopefully, both of them together could care for their older brother when I grow old.

When Lan was fifteen months old, I learned I was pregnant with my third and last child. My pregnancy would be uneventful, although I did undergo a litany of tests similar to my previous pregnancies. Being pregnant again was supposed to be a joyful event since Lan would soon be having a new sibling with whom to play, and my husband and I both wanted to increase her social interaction. However, the happiness was short-lived, and the relationship with my husband deteriorated further. Sometimes he apologized for not being there when I needed him the most, but his words and actions did not correlate.

Every couple of weeks, we would make the drive to Poughkeepsie, NY, to attend a quick counseling session with a psychiatrist to discuss our son's condition as well as his medication. On the way home, sometimes the ongoing, underlying tension between us escalated into heated arguments. Times like these, I felt like I was outside in the snow or inside the freezer: cold and numb to it all. At the time, I did not know and no one had mentioned to me about any supporting services except the schooling and resources for Nam. I didn't know there were services for parents of autistic kids as well. We definitely could have used them!

Many times while pregnant with my third child, I was alone caring for my son and my toddler daughter. One icy and snowy early morning while the children were asleep, still in my nightgown and slippers, I sat close to the window and peeked outside. The snow was so thick that it covered the front lawn like a white blanket that encircled our house. The icicles formed on the roof eaves normally look picturesque to me, but not that morning. They looked just like an upside-down picket fences, but the pickets seemed more like tentacles at times moving as though they were reaching out and grasping at my lonely soul.

I felt trapped in a dead end with no way out. Like a ship with no sails, a boat with no oars, it floats aimlessly at the mercy of the wind and the water. I thought about leaving my husband and bringing the children back to my family in Southern California. A soft voice took me by surprise, "Where's Daddy?" I turned around, and my daughter was right behind me clutching a Barney plush doll in her arms. Then I thought about my daughter who adored her Daddy, and how leaving my husband would affect her. I also thought about the heavy burden and the tremendous stress I would bring to my parents if I showed up at their home with my children. I would never want to be a burden to anyone, least of all to my parents. With tears in my eyes, I extinguished that thought and hugged Lan. The snow continued to cover our house, the ice continued to form underneath the snow, and the wind continued to howl.

CHAPTER 9

MY YOUNGEST CHILD

– BETWEEN HOPE AND HEARTACHE

My younger daughter was born a healthy baby, 8 pounds, 9 ounces via a normal delivery in 1995. We named her Mai, a Vietnamese New Year flower. I did not have the "almost roadside delivery" problem I had when I delivered Lan. The contractions were regular, came gradually, and thus I had ample time to get to the hospital.

After Mai's arrival, I decided to leave work permanently to care for my children. Sometimes I asked my husband if we could hire someone, now that we had three children and especially with our son's situation. He told me I should go back to work because we could not afford to hire someone on just one salary. There were days, though, I felt I was stretched too thin in my daily tasks as a mother and housekeeper, and I had a hard time juggling everything and maintaining my energy and sanity. In short, I was physically and emotionally drained.

Every day I focused on teaching Lan while caring for Nam and Mai. Mai was only a few weeks old but she slept through the night. She had a beautiful face and smile. Like Lan, I also breastfed Mai but added bottle supplements. Her infant growth and development appeared normal. I felt hopeful about her progress and developmental milestones.

Nam continued to go to Children's Annex in Kingston, although he was making little progress. In fact, his crying episodes had increased in frequency and intensity. In 1996, we took him to the UCLA Neuropsychiatric Institute and Hospital for a consultation, and he underwent a second brain MRI at UCI Medical Center/MRI Center. The result of this repeated MRI was normal once again.

Because he sucked his thumb constantly and chewed on items indiscriminately, he became sick with colds or bronchitis several times year and even had pneumonia during the winter on occasion. One time he came home with a Coxsackie virus infection. He also had diarrhea many times due to his constant chewing of non-food items. I loved my son so much, yet there was little I could do for him. Sometimes, in agonizing moments when I felt I couldn't reach or help him, a big chunk of my heart went with him to whatever place he seemed to be disappearing.

In 1996, my husband was able to transfer to IBM in San Jose, California, where the climate is a lot warmer in the winter, and more programs existed for the care of my son. Anticipating that the change might improve Nam's condition, I was so excited and began to pack and prepare for the move. However, my happiness was short-lived.

A couple of weeks before we started our move, I noticed changes in Lan's behavior. Besides the poor eye contact and echolalia, she also began to show fear of certain things, such as noises, that had not seemed to bother her before. For example, one day her father was sleeping, and she heard his snoring. She screamed and made me close the door. Another time, we were at the mall when she heard the fire engine sounds; she started to cry. The kitchen faucet leaked, and she could not bear hearing the water droplets. We would be outside playing, and she would start crying and running back into the house because she had felt a breeze on her face or arms.

The rain and wind terrified her. On a windy and drizzling summer afternoon, I needed to take her with me on an errand, but she refused to go out unless I put a sweatshirt on her that covered most of her head, face and arms. Even then, she began her anxiety again after only a few minutes.

She also began to feel afraid of having her picture taken or being near a camera. We thought these fears might be temporary and could be caused by anxiety related to the move. We hoped they would pass once we settled down in California.

CHAPTER 10

THE MOVE FROM NEW YORK

TO CALIFORNIA

Although we'd moved before, this particular relocation felt quite difficult for me. I brought my children to my parents' house in Southern California for a visit while my husband was still in New York taking care of the house and preparing for the move. At that time, Nam was about eight years old; Lan had just turned three, and Mai was just one year old. My husband travelled with us on the airplane but heading back to the East Coast shortly after we arrived to California. Lan cried constantly and refused to go to the bathroom the entire time we were on the plane. Nam also cried off and on during the flight. When we arrived at the rental car place approximately eight hours later, we brought out Lan's little port-a-potty, and she finally was able to urinate.

I found it extremely difficult to stay at my parents' home with my son's constant crying and Lan's incessant fear of the rain and wind. At the time, my parents were old and not always in good health, and I felt that I was creating additional stress and burden on them. My siblings also had families and problems of their own with which to deal.

One day my son cried so hard he experienced an excessively bloody nose. I remember my mom frantically driving us to the emergency room. I was caring for him and signing consent papers while holding my younger daughter in my arm. Nam had to have a second nasal cauterization under general anesthesia in Anaheim Memorial Hospital in 1996.

When my nieces and nephews came over for a visit, they were curious about Nam's behaviors and eccentricities as well as his crying. They always asked me, "What's wrong with him?" "How come he can't talk?" or "Why does he cry all the time?" They also were puzzled by my daughter's behaviors. They asked, "Why is she afraid of the rain and the wind?" "Why is she afraid of the camera?" "How come she talks funny?" I tried to explain to them about autism, but they were too young to understand. Eventually my children and I moved to a hotel so we wouldn't disrupt other members of the family who needed their sleep so they could go to work rested. My husband later came to the hotel and drove us up to San Jose, where we stayed at the Residence Inn in Sunnyvale, California temporarily while we looked for a house.

At first, we thought we would rent an apartment, but my son's constant crying episodes and Lan's screaming outbursts due to her phobias made it difficult for us to be in such close quarters with other people. We decided that owning a house would be a better option. We thought we would only have to stay at the hotel temporarily — a few weeks at most, but we end up living there for about 8 months because of our children's situation and the housing market at the time. The staff at the Residence Inn was very understanding, and they gave us the special discounted long-term stay rate. They also did not place any guests in the room next to ours because of the noise our children made.

One time, when a technician came in to our room to check the fire alarm, Lan screamed hysterically. Her face turned purplish red, and it took a while for her to calm down. I thought the loud noise of the fire alarm startled and frightened her. However, I noted in my journal that Lan was fearful of fire alarm noises, in addition to the fire engine sound, dripping water noise from the faucet, snoring, the rain, the wind, camera, windshield wipers, etc.

The rainy season was particularly difficult for all of us. Lan refused to go out when it was windy or rainy, even if it was just a small drizzle. If it started to rain suddenly while we were already in the car, we had to stop the car and wait until the rain stopped or wait until Lan fell asleep. Turning on the windshield wipers terrified her as well. A trip anywhere with them would be quite exhaustive for me. Besides frequent outbursts and meltdowns from the children while we were driving, Nam also had difficulty sitting still in the car. Sometimes he unbuckled the belt and moved around. Other times, he repeatedly rocked, chewed on the seat belt or self-stimulated. I redirected his attention to other activities and even taped a small toy on his shirt to reduce his self-stimulation, but even this did not seem to work well.

Using the address at the Residence Inn, we were able to register Nam at Cherry Chase Elementary in Sunnyvale. Every day, the school bus picked him up from the Residence Inn and brought him to school. I requested a "buckle lock" for Nam because I knew he would unbuckle his belt and try to move around. Nam's teacher, Mrs. H., and the classroom aides exhibited incredible patience with Nam, especially during his crying episodes.

We also brought him to a neurologist and pediatrician who prescribed new medication. At that time, we were more concerned about Nam's situation and his safety. We thought Lan's sudden fears were triggered by the moving anxiety and that she would eventually outgrow them once she got adjusted to her new environment. Drug therapy for Lan did not cross our minds at this point.

Mai also was beginning to show delays in her speech and language skills; she rarely babbled, gestured or imitated, despite my repeated prompting. At twenty-months old, she was unable to say a single intelligible word. She also enjoyed rocking and fixating on one activity repeatedly. However, she did not appear to have any other autistic features — social, phobic, or behavioral challenges – at this point.

In the evening, my husband would go with a realtor friend to look for houses. We took a loss selling our house in New York, and with our one-salary budget, it took a while for us to find a reasonably priced, good house in the Santa Clara County area. About eight months after arriving in California, we stumbled on a house we really liked that also offered favorable purchasing incentives and reasonable financing. It was a single story, ranch-style house located in Los Gatos, situated conveniently near the elementary school, park, and supermarket. Although it sat on a relatively busy road, the house had a fenced-in yard and a gate. The house needed some repairs and improvements including a new furnace. Regardless, my daughters and I fell in love with this house. Years later, Lan told me that Los Gatos is her "hometown." Moving to this area opened a new chapter in my life and in my children's lives.

CHAPTER 11

LOS GATOS, CA

– THE CHANGES AND THE CHALLENGES

It took some time for us to move all our boxes from storage to our new home in Los Gatos, California, in 1997 and settle in. Once unpacked, I had to begin finding the children's appropriate schools and services. I would also eventually need to address Lan's phobias.

Not long after the boxes were unpacked, someone recommended that we contact the San Andreas Regional Center (SARC) about services to help our children. Indeed, it turned out they could help, and they provided support programs for Nam, and later on Lan. Even though Nam was eligible for respite services, I did not use any service hours for close to two years because I was afraid of the stigma.

Caring for my children and the constant wailing from Nam, eventually took a toll on me physically and psychologically. Sometimes, I walked out of the house looking like a zombie. Out of exhaustion, I contacted the agency again and began to use the service as needed. All of my children became clients of SARC.

Nam was nine years old when we first moved to Los Gatos. Lan was four, and Mai was two years old. Nam continued to attend Cherry Chase Elementary school for one more year before starting at McKinnon Autism School. At this time, we knew the challenges we faced with Nam, and despite Lan's poor eye contact, echolalia, and phobias, and Mai's speech and language delays, we were still hanging on to a tiny thread of hope that Lan and Mai would improve. With that in mind, we planned to register Lan for a local preschool, Growing Footprints, before starting her in kindergarten at Blossom Hill Elementary School. We hoped that the preschool environment would prepare her well for the kindergarten school year.

Eventually, however, we had to face the truth. Within months of enrolling Lan in preschool, we realized that both Lan and Mai definitely displayed signs and symptoms of Autism Spectrum Disorders (ASD). They needed help — the sooner the better. At home, I focused tremendous effort on helping Lan to adjust to the new house, environment, and school as well as helping Mai with verbal communication. Sometimes I took Lan and Mai to see other kids in the neighborhood to improve their social and communication skills.

The house had to be arranged in a specific way to accommodate Nam's severe autism. There were no steps, stairs, sharp objects, plants, and literally no furniture at all anywhere except the living room. Even then, those items could not be bulky or heavy. Pens, pencils, and other small items were usually stashed away in a drawer because my son would chew them. Every room had a phone, a first-aid kit or first aid essentials, flashlight, baby wipes, diapers, and paper towels all tucked away in a cabinet with a safety latch. I selected toys that were educational with no small, removable parts or lead paint on them and kept them in a plastic container in the living room. I used large three-drawer plastic storage carts to store their clothes.

The children's bedroom — the master bedroom — had no bed frames or headboards on the beds, only mattresses, because my son could hurt himself during crying episodes. We had to replace many mattresses because Nam and Mai would rock constantly on them and wear them out quickly. At night Nam required diapers despite his age, and inevitably these diapers would leak. I spent a lot of time in the children's room to ensure their safety as well as to teach them and monitor their progress and setbacks.

69

As Lan got older, she wanted her own room. We accommodated her by carefully re-organizing the rest of the house, so that every child essentially had their own room according to their needs. This included a separate calming/comforting room for Nam that had a mattress on the floor, well-padded with pillows and blankets to prevent him from hurting himself during the crying episodes. Soft music played in the room for him to listen, and I placed a baby monitor there so I could hear him around the house. If Nam's crying episodes intensified and frightened his sisters, I would take him there temporarily until he calmed down. I could leave him there alone and listen to him on the monitor; however, I always checked on him every 5-10 minutes to be sure he didn't hurt himself or have a bloody nose. Sometimes Nam would fall asleep in this room.

When the children were young, I used laminated flashcards and pictures to teach them. Every night, after brushing their teeth, I used these flashcards to teach my younger daughter, Mai, and I also reviewed some of the math, reading, and spelling concepts with Lan. I remember Mai could not pronounce A, B, or C; the sounds that came out of her mouth were "Cha, Cha, Ah" for each letter. Even at four years old, she had difficulty articulating and sounding out simple words such as book, pencil, pen, open, shoe, cat, mom, or dad. She could not speak in phrases or full sentences until she was around six or seven years old.

Like Lan, Mai was also afraid of certain things, such as wind, rain, and flying bugs. There were times Mai constantly rocked on a chair while playing on the computer; other times, she vocalized for stimulation, mumbled or hummed some unintelligible words (Si Ho Ho Si Wee) or sounds while staring at something on the wall. For a long time, she seemed obsessed with my elbow. She would constantly sit by my side and put my elbow on her cheek, nose, or mouth. Her lack of focus and short attention span also made it difficult for me to read a book or play a game with her. When she learned to walk, she walked on her toes. This has never changed and is actually one of the characteristics recognized in autistic children.

In 1998, the pediatric neurologist, Dr. K., ordered an MRI of the brain, tests for Fragile X syndrome, and a chromosomal analysis study for Mai. The results were found to be within normal limits. I noticed that the findings in Mai's MRI were very similar to the findings in Nam's MRI:

"There are several tiny, scattered foci of increased signal intensity on T2 weighted images in the deep white matter..."

The following is from Nam's MRI finding:

"A few punctuate areas of abnormal high signal on the T2 weighted images are noted in the deep white matter..."

One day, I noticed that Mai was pulling out the toys from the plastic container and lining them in a straight line from the living room to the kitchen. I took one item out of the straight line and noticed she did not cry or try to pull it out of my hand. She did not even look at me; instead, she searched in her toy container for another item to replace the one I had taken. I put all the toys away and only put out one or two that both of us could play with together. Eventually, she stopped lining things up. This tendency to align objects would also be recognized as a trait of autism in children.

Sometimes I called her name, and she would look at me but sometimes she would look elsewhere. Yet, her hearing test was normal. Since her speech was not improving, I tried to bring her to the speech therapist at Blossom Hill Elementary School, where she was now a student, but she adamantly refused to attend the session with the therapist; she fought hard and screamed loudly.

Through my husband's insurance, we had a speech therapist, Ms. CJ R., come to our house twice a week to help Mai for about two years. (We paid 20 percent of the total cost.) Mai was very fond of her and seemed to improve a lot. CJ was very patient and dedicated. She would try different methods to help Mai improve in her communication as well as her social skills. I consider CJ one of the heroes in Mai's life. Mai also was enrolled in the Special Day Program Pre-school at Discovery School before attending the Special Day Class at Blossom Hill Elementary School. For a while, despite the deficits in communication and social skills, Mai did not have significant behavioral issues.

We briefly hired a woman for several months to help with the kids. Even though the babysitter did not have transportation and did not speak English well, she treated my children well and helped me considerably. I was in the process of training her so that I could go back to work part-time and help with the family budget, but the children's conditions had gotten worse at times; thus, I decided to stay home a bit longer. Soon after, the babysitter moved to a different state and started a small business.

At this time, Lan continued to have certain phobias, obsessive interests, and difficulty accepting even minor changes. One day we were on our way to a familiar scenic drive when her father had to take a detour because of road construction. She started to scream in the car. "It's okay, Lan!" we told her. "We'll take you to Denny's for ice cream." We thought surely this would ease her fear and anxiety and calm her down since it was her favorite treat, but she continued crying all the way to Denny's. Once we arrived at the restaurant, the waitress gave her candy and ice cream, but she could not be calmed. Her crying did not even stop when we got home.

At home, I had a tough time changing things around the house. Lan screamed when I replaced her pillowcase or her favorite rose blanket with a new one. If she noted that I changed the location of a lamp, she immediately put it back to where it was. If I rearranged the books on the table, she immediately put them back to the way they were previously. She became upset and repeatedly asked me, "Why did you change...?" It did not matter how I responded or what reasons I gave, she continued to ask the same question over and over again. I had to find ways to distract her from the repetitive questioning and fixations.

We took her to the neurologist, Dr. K., who suggested medication that appeared to improve the behaviors somewhat. We tried both medication and behavior modification with moderate success. Under stress, however, Lan's autistic traits resurfaced.

Over the years, it seemed that she had one obsessive interest after another. First, there was Eeyore from *Winnie the Pooh*, then Barney, Arthur, Lemur, then a bug, dog, puppy, or cat. She could sit for a while watching a TV program or doing an activity that she was interested in. She enjoyed watching *Arthur* repeatedly and even wrote a mini-short story about Arthur. However, she would easily be distracted by changes, new concepts, certain noises, certain sounds, bugs, flying insects, crowded places, or even the weather, so that focusing on learning new or unfamiliar concepts would be difficult. This was especially true of abstract thinking, and things that did not immediately follow a pattern, or did not seem to "fit" or "click," especially in the area of reading comprehension.

At times I also was afraid for her safety. I remember one afternoon at the park, I saw her following a woman who was walking with a puppy toward her car. I immediately ran after her, called her name several times, and finally she turned around. When she finally acknowledged me, she looked like she had just woken up.

One summer we had an ant problem in the kitchen. I recall a particular afternoon when I was exhausted from cleaning the kitchen to deter the ants and trying to get rid of them. However, Lan kept returning from the front yard with a cup in her hand filled with ants. She told me that those ants were her pets and I should not get rid of them. It took me a while to convince her ants and bugs were not her pets.

While both my daughters had certain repetitive behaviors, fixations, and fears, Lan was more pronounced in her fears of eye contact, new environments, certain noises, cameras, and windshield wipers. Over the years, with early intervention, behavior modification, medication, and specialized education programs, some of their autistic features have improved but some have remained. Looking back, it seems that most of my children's autistic features began to appear, or at least became prominent, between the ages of two and four years of age. While at Growing Footprints preschool, Lan had problems with anxiety and would not let her instructor out of sight. She rarely socialized with other children and cried constantly.

During kindergarten at Blossom Hill elementary, Lan's teacher noted that she exhibited certain odd behaviors. She was afraid of going to assemblies, crowded places, places with loud music, and classes with a substitute teacher. She was distracted and bothered by certain noises, plus she was unable to sit down for long and concentrate on her work. Lan would roam around the classroom at times, and she had problem looking at people's faces while carrying on a conversation. She also repeated things not pertinent to the conversation or class activities. One day she was really upset and cried because she had to wait outside after the bell rang because of painting being done in the classroom. She told the teacher that she had to be in the classroom exactly after the morning bell rang.

The school staff invited me to meet with her teacher and the school psychologist, who would later perform a psychoanalysis report. Academically, Lan seemed to be at the same level with her peers, yet she had tremendous challenges in communication and social development. Eventually, she was transferred to the Special Education Class, which at Blossom Hill was called the Special Day Class.

One day, I asked my husband to come along on her class field trip as a chaperone to keep an eye on Lan because we knew her behaviors and phobia too well and how they could flare up in any number of situations. Both of them came home together unexpectedly; she was crying and he was upset. I asked what happened, and he told me that when Lan saw one of the parents taking pictures of her child with a camera, she freaked out and screamed. My husband put a camera around her neck, and she started to scream again and threw the camera on the sofa. After that, we let her play with the camera repeatedly for a long time, and gradually she was able to conquer her fear of cameras and took her first picture — of the ceiling. By the time she reached six or seven years old, her fear of cameras diminished.

At the beginning of first grade, Lan was able to join the mainstream regular classroom with an aide to assist her when she was having problems or meltdowns. She also started one medication after another (Buspar, Elavil, etc.). She did not last long on each because of the severe side effects she experienced. At times, she was nauseated, chewed on her hair, chewed on her fingernails, fidgeted a lot, and still had significant problems focusing. Several months after switching her medication to Prozac, however, we noted a significant improvement. The anxiety incidents seemed to lessen, and it reduced her obsession with sameness and routine as well. She was able to focus more. She also seemed to benefit significantly from a structured environment and the assistance of her dedicated classroom aide, Ms. J.M., whom Lan referred to as Ms. J.

Throughout her elementary and middle school years, Ms. J. became instrumental in Lan's progress. My daughter would not have turned out the way she did if not for the love and patience of Ms. J. Over the years Lan became very fond of her, and we are grateful to have had her in our lives.

Lan seemed to have trouble expressing her feelings or understanding other people's feelings. She did not understand jokes or social cues. These factors would make it difficult for Lan to have and retain friends. Every day, Ms. J. would find different ways to help Lan express her feelings and reduce her incidences of crying and impulsivity. When Lan was having meltdowns and began to cry or show disruptive behaviors in class, Ms. J. would walk with Lan around the school and talk to her. She also taped a 3x5 card on Lan's desk to remind her of appropriate behaviors in class. I think of Ms. J. as another hero who helped my daughter.

If there was a turning point in Lan's life, I would say it was during third grade at Blossom Hill Elementary School. My husband and I were going through a difficult time in our relationship, and it seemed that an imminent divorce was inevitable. Lan also was starting to have more academic and social problems. One afternoon, she came home crying. She told me she was having a hard time making friends and that someone was teasing her. In addition, she also was having difficulty with multiplication tables. I literally dropped what I was doing and began working with her on multiplication tables as well as addressing the social interaction problems she was having. Within a week, she could recite all the multiplication tables with speed and precision.

At Lan's Individual Educational Plan (IEP) meeting with the teachers and staff, I made sure that her social deficits and phobias were the primary focus of the IEP meeting. In fact, during this meeting, Mrs. P., the principal at Blossom Hill Elementary School at that time, made a suggestion that changed our lives forever. The teacher noted that my daughter seemed easily distracted and seemed to have problems looking into people's face while carrying on a conversation. She also was afraid of loud music, hand-clapping, and sirens. Many times she had difficulty with jokes and social cues and repeated certain things out of context. Together we tried to brainstorm and figure out a way to improve Lan's social and communication skills.

Mrs. P. asked me what Lan's hobbies were, and I told her she liked to play on the computer, sing, listen to music, and watch TV programs such as *Barney* and *Arthur*. She thought for a moment then asked, "Can Lan join Choir?"

Choir required Lan being at rehearsal early in the morning, and getting her there would be a bit difficult for me since I had to care for Mai and prepare Nam for his school. It also coincided with Nam's busing schedule. To make it possible for Lan to join choir, Mrs. P. offered to come by in the morning to pick Lan up and take her to rehearsal since we lived close to the school. Choir had already started and usually students had to audition to get into choir, but Mrs. P. assured me she would talk to the teacher about Lan's unique situation. Later that day, she spoke to Lan and mentioned the choir class and the practice. Lan seemed very excited about this prospect, and that evening, joining Choir was all that was on Lan's mind.

Lan enjoyed Choir, and getting involved in this activity changed her tremendously. It presented new opportunities for Lan to grow and overcome her condition. For example, she was sup-posed to go on a choir field trip, but she told me she wanted to stay home because the weather forecast predicted a windy, rainy day. (She was still afraid of the rain.) I told her that many of her friends would be on this trip and they might want to hang out with her af-terwards. In addition, the choir teacher would be upset if Lan did not show up. Somehow it worked. She tried hard, and gradually she was able to reduce her fear of the wind and rain.

As she became more sociable, she also became less afraid of eye contact and loud noises. She loved performing on stage in front of a crowd. Choir also broadened her horizon as she traveled to many places for performances. In 2006, while in seventh grade, Lan even traveled to New York and appeared outside of the NBC Today show taping.

Lan clearly broke out of her shell and even made moderate progress in terms of friendship while in choir. Music and stage performance became her interests. "Mom, I want to be a singer or actress when I grow up." She told me she would like to become a singer someday. She continued choir throughout elementary school, middle school, and up to her ninth grade in high school. In addition to medication (Prozac), I think choir, friendship, and behavior modification made a significant difference in terms of reducing Lan's most prominent autistic features — phobias, echolalia, obsession, impulsivity, resistance to change, and lack of eye contact.

Even though choir helped her tremendously, Lan still had problems expressing her feelings as well as understanding other people's feelings and interpreting social cues. She did not understand that her friends needed "space" and became sad and upset if they talked and laughed with someone else. Also, her inability to understand jokes caused misunderstanding with her friends. When people laughed at a joke, she thought they were laughing at her. Ms. J. was wonderful in helping Lan with this problem. Sometimes Lan inadvertently blurted out things that were not pertinent to a conversation or situation, which also made it difficult for her to get along with others.

While Lan was progressing at her schools, I knew that Nam was having difficulty at his schools. I drove to McKinnon Autism School a few times to visit with him. After I parked the car, I could hear his loud cry echoing, even from the parking lot. Sometimes I gathered the courage to go into the classroom. Other times I just sat in the car sobbing, and then I drove home feeling empty and sad.

Several weeks into Nam's first school year at McKinnon, an aggressive student bit him on the upper arm twice. I requested that he be transferred to Hazelwood Elementary School/Severely Handicapped County Program. Occasionally, the school bus driver told me Nam cried so hard that she had to stop the bus and thus she dropped him off to school or home a little later than usual. Even though he was on medication, his crying episodes continued.

Late one afternoon, Nam cried until he was so exhausted he fell asleep on the living room couch. I slowly and gingerly brought him to the bedroom and put him on his mattress. I lied down next to my daughters who were also sleeping soundly. I felt a tremendous sense of sadness and desperation come over me —that parental feeling when as a mother you know you cannot do anything to alleviate the pain and suffering of your child, physically or psychologically. I wept softly, afraid to wake up my children.

At this time, I knew my younger daughter showed many signs and symptoms of ASD, too. Through my tears, I silently screamed and asked God/Buddha, *Why...Why...Why me?* I thought about some women who were drunk, did drugs, or smoked throughout their pregnancy, and yet their children were okay. I thought about my friend's infant daughter who was born prematurely and had to stay in the hospital for months, but she turned out just fine. *I did not smoke, drink, or take drugs, so what happened? I feel like I lost my son when he was around five years old and could not get him back. Could it be that I would eventually lose my daughters, too? All I had asked for was to have an ordinary family: a husband who loved and cared for me, children who could talk and behave normally and go to school just like all the other children. Was this too much to ask?*

There were days I pulled out all my notes and the children's records to search for answers. What could have caused their autism? Could it be the thiomersal, mercury-based preservative in the vaccines they received? Could it be the MMR vaccine? Could it be genetic or environmental factors or both? The search for answers only brought more questions and doubts. My mom had eleven children, and I have more than a dozen nieces and nephews, but none had the disease. None of my husband's siblings or his siblings' children had this disease either. There was no evidence of genetic linkage either on his side or on my side of the family.

The only answer in which I could find comfort was that of fate, love, and acceptance. Yet, this was not easy at all, and the feeling of acceptance is similar to someone who resigns to her fate of being shipwrecked and stranded alone on a remote deserted island. Once again, I was surrounded by water and I must somehow fight for survival in the vast Pacific Ocean. I must survive for the sake of my children. *The war was over long ago; why am I not at peace?* I wondered. *There are no more bombings and gunfire. Why am I still having overwhelming feelings of devastation?*

At times, I asked for guidance from God/Buddha. One night I could not sleep, so I turned on the TV. I did not know what channel I was watching because my eyes were full of tears. Then something caught my attention, and I immediately wiped my eyes. It was a talk show program where a man who recently lost his daughter due to an illness shared his thoughts with an audience. The interviewer asked if he wanted to say anything to all the parents out there, and fighting back tears, he said, "Please hug your child...No matter what, you still have your child to hug and to hold. I don't have...anymore..."

In that moment I felt as if I just woke up. I had been questioning fate and fighting a war within myself. I went into my children's bedroom and looked at my sleeping children and actually smiled. I had not lost them. They were still there with me. They may have been difficult and challenging due to their autism, but they were still my children. They did not choose to be autistic. I gently held my children's hands while they slept.

From that day on, I no longer asked God, "Why me?" I told myself, "Why not me?" I believe I have a good heart, a good upbringing, and I am resilient enough that I can take on the challenge. I can give them the love and care they need. I gave birth to them and will always love and care for them regardless of what disease they have or what conditions they are in. I believe someone from above told me not to despair at this time when my world appeared to be falling apart.

From this point forward I chose something positive, some accomplishments that my children could do, even minor ones like remembering to flush the toilet or turn on or off the light and focused on this every day. This provided me with my happiness. Some days there were more setbacks than successes, more bad news than good news, including intense arguments with my husband. Times like these I would step outside to breathe some fresh air, watch the sun rise, hear the birds chipping, feel the breeze, and remind myself that life is precious and beautiful. We are all put on this earth for a reason — to do something positive and meaningful. I must overcome obstacles and bumps on the road if I am going to travel far.

I focused tremendous energy into helping all my children but especially my middle daughter, Lan. I was encouraged by her slow but steady progress in school and at home. I believed she had the best chance of leading a "close to normal life" and hopefully could take care of her older brother and younger sister when I grow old. That was my goal then and is still my goal now.

After trying various medications including pain medications, Nam's neurologist eventually started him on Prozac. Several months later, I noticed a change in his crying episodes. The frequency was a bit less and the intensity reduced. Although we tried various medications for Lan and Mai, the one that seemed to help significantly with the least side effects was Prozac. In fact, all of my children have been on Prozac and are currently taking Prozac daily.

Nam's special education teacher, Mr. S.S., at Hazelwood, came to my house and gave us an old MAC computer that had specialized programs, such as "First Thousand Words," that really benefited Mai's language skills. When he finished hooking up the computer, he taught her how to use it. She was afraid to touch the mouse, but he calmed her down and said, "Don't worry, this is not the real mouse...it won't bite you..." After a few weeks, my daughter started enjoying her computer usage, and she started repeating some of the phrases in the program.

Although I don't recommend kids using computers constantly, I have to credit Mai's computer experience with her improvement in speech, reading, and writing. Mr. S.S.'s teaching assistant in class, Mr. J.H., helped Nam a lot in school, and sometimes during the weekend, he came and helped me with Nam under the respite care program.

Nam's next school was Dartmouth Middle School and then on to Castro Middle School. Mai continued at Blossom Hill Elementary School Special Day Class. In our fragile state, it has always been the extraordinary care and compassion that the professionals at the children's schools have exhibited that has made all the difference. I have always been grateful for the tireless efforts of all the teachers, aides, and staff.

When I think about my children's schooling, placement, and services (including the IEPs), I think about one special person, a program specialist for Los Gatos Union School District, Mrs. J.M. I will always be grateful to her for all that she did to help my children over the years. Even though she was old and not in good health, and there were times she walked into the meeting with a cane, she did her best to stand up for those who cannot stand up and lend a voice to those who have no voice. Every autistic child needs someone like her on their side.

CHAPTER 12

THE DIVORCE – THE END

AND THE BEGINNING

Towards 2001, when my older daughter Lan was about eight years old, my relationship with my husband reached a boiling point. Although he and I argued frequently, we both made an effort not to argue in front of the children. During the week, he would come home for dinner and go straight to the bedroom to do work, watch TV, movies, or surf the internet. When I complained that he did not spend enough time with his children, he brushed it off and said, "I'm tired."

On the weekends, however, my husband would take the children to a restaurant and then around to various local natural places and parks so they could look at the hills, grassy land, lakes, ducks, cows, and deer. Occasionally we drove up the mountains and looked down at the beautiful scenery. Sometimes Lan and Mai wanted to go to Santa Cruz or to the movies, and he took the girls there. However, for a while we did not take Nam to any restaurants because of his frequent outbursts and crying episodes. After trying Prozac, it seemed his crying episodes were less frequent, and he was able to enjoy going out a bit more. Thus, we started taking all the children to restaurants again. If we were out, as soon as Nam started to cry I would take him back to the car and sit there with him. We tried this a few times, and it seemed to work out well. Eventually he was able to sit still in a restaurant, mostly rocking, vocalizing, and playing with his hands but with few crying episodes.

One afternoon, I was in a restaurant with Nam when he started to cry, and my husband complained, "It was you who wanted to eat in a restaurant...His crying bothered other customers...It was you..." I had had it and sadly responded, "You know, if you don't want to take him out, that's fine. I will go out with anyone who loves my son and is not embarrassed to be seen with him." Perhaps I tried to get his attention with that comment or elicit a response from him that would help me understand his indifference.

I admit it was sometimes difficult to take Nam out. Once, on the Santa Cruz beach boardwalk, I was holding Nam's hand as we headed back to the car. A young teenage boy passed us with a milkshake cup in his hand. Suddenly, Nam grabbed the cup and drank. He did this so quickly that I was unable to stop him. I tried to explain, apologized, and offered to buy a new one for the boy, but he refused and did not seem upset.

During an outing, a couple of families were having a picnic at the park when Nam ran toward them and picked up a piece of watermelon. Another time, Nam and I were in a hotel lobby having breakfast. I was standing in line with Nam trying to get him some food. I was holding his right hand with my left hand and holding a plate with my right hand. A woman passed by with a plate of bacon and eggs, and suddenly Nam reached out quickly and grabbed two pieces of bacon off her plate and put them in his mouth. I turned around and apologized. She smiled and said, "That's okay. Don't worry about it. I worked with autistic children..."

One Thanksgiving we took Nam and the children out to Marie Callender's Restaurant. We usually go to Olive Garden for special occasions, but it was too crowded that day. While waiting, Nam vocalized and rocked so severely on a chair that he almost tipped the chair over. Lan was not patient and constantly complained about the wait. Mai looked around and began to talk to herself. I constantly reminded my son about the rocking and held his arm to prevent him from tipping. Suddenly, the waitress came over and told us that a family had just moved to another table so we could have their seats. When we asked for the bill, the waitress told us that an anonymous family had just paid our bill. We were pleasantly surprised, but most of all it affirmed that compassionate people still existed in the world. Their gesture of good will warmed our hearts and brightened our spirits that holiday.

Sometimes, I had to take Nam to the supermarket with me. This always turned out to be quite an experience. I remembered making pho, and I ran out of bean sprouts and cilantro. I could have asked my husband to get it after work but figured it was not worth the bother. I packed Nam in the car and drove to Lunardi's supermarket, the closest supermarket near our house. As soon as I got in line at the express checkout lane, he started to suck his thumb and cry. A small boy in the other aisle was staring at him; I guess he probably never saw a thirteen-year-old boy sucking his thumb and crying before. A few customers also stared at him, and soon all eyes were on him. There were six people ahead of me, and all of them told me to go ahead.

I experienced many other similar situations. Each time people responded with kindness and understanding, and I felt fortunate to live in a community where such a response was not only possible but common.

After we brought the children back home from their usual weekend outings (eating brunch, feeding the ducks, sightseeing, or browsing the Barnes and Noble bookstore), their father would disappear to be alone — he'd either go to the bedroom or go back out. Aside from the several hours during our weekend excursions, it seemed he had no other desire to spend time with the children, and he helped very little, if at all, with their care or with any household tasks in general. I spent all my time taking care of my children — day and night — in addition to doing all the household chores. I was always alone. Day after day, night after night, nothing changed. As time went on, I accepted this fact and rarely asked him for help with anything. With the growing distance between us, it was impossible to have a warm, close or intimate relationship with my husband.

The echo of our arguments then became the writing on the wall. Our life was filled by our war of words: dull and dry, empty and explicit, blunt and bleak, tangy and tawdry. The constant blaming and barrage of criticism also formed a built-in brick wall in our relationship. As solid as that wall seemed, it also was as ready to break as rubber band stretched to its limits. I believe the children's condition was just a factor, albeit a big factor, in my failing marriage that magnified the vast differences between my husband and me. Looking back now, I see the end coming like watching a movie where the audience senses the foreshadowing of the conclusion: the ending is inevitable.

On a particular Saturday night when my husband came home very late, a terrific argument ensued, and I resolved that it would be the last one in our marriage. We both truly believed that the best thing for us was to *end* the marriage and not to *mend* it. How could we salvage something that was never there? From the beginning our relationship — our marriage — was lacking the essential elements necessary to succeed, even without the stress of raising three autistic children. I had no regret about my decision. I just knew I had nothing to salvage. There were no more ultimatums to ponder and no more arguments to counter. This was a decision I should have made years earlier. His reaction was one that I had expected, and it mirrored the pattern of apathy I had grown accustomed to.

After we agreed to proceed with the divorce, there were nights I stayed up late thinking about the uncertainty of our future; I had trouble sleeping and wept frequently. *What will happen to my children?* I wondered. Would he continue to support his children (at least until they turned 18 years old)? Or would he just take off when all the paperwork was completed? Would I be strong enough to pick up the pieces and move on?

All the years we were married, besides the financial support, I sensed that he was giving nothing else to the marriage and participated very little to the upbringing of the children. So I concluded, *maybe it is best that I now have the peace of mind to care for them, and perhaps, he has the freedom to pursue his interests and forge a new life for himself. Now it's just a formality — a piece of legal document to end 15 years of marriage. The burden is on my shoulders; how should I proceed with the divorce and, most importantly, how would I keep our children's lives the least disruptive as possible?*

At first, my husband told me to start looking for a lawyer to represent me, because he would get one to represent him. I made appointments with a few lawyers for a free estimate, and I was amazed at how much it would cost — way beyond what I could afford — to get divorced. Then one day, I was at the Barnes and Noble bookstore and a book caught my eyes, *How to Do a Divorce in California*. I purchased the book for $34.99 and began to read it carefully line by line. Every day after dropping my daughters at school, I went to Denny's to have some breakfast and continued to read the book. I could not bear going home and feeling the emptiness. Besides, for some reason, I could read and absorb better in a restaurant or a coffee shop.

It was difficult at first because the book contained so many legal terms that I did not understand. Eventually I was able to assemble all the required forms as well as the settlement agreement on my own to proceed with the divorce. I have to admit the book helped me tremendously, and I would recommend it to anyone who is going through a divorce. The bottom line was that I wanted to ensure that my children would be well taken care of and that this separation/divorce would have minimal impact on them.

When I presented my husband with the settlement agreement, he agreed, with very little opposition to the terms. Our divorce proceedings went relatively smoothly, and we filed all the required forms with the court. Shortly after the divorce was finalized, my ex-husband mentioned that he would have to move to New York for job stability. He also asked if I wanted to bring the children to New York. I declined for obvious reasons. He granted me sole custody of the children; he agreed to financial obligations and a flexible visitation schedule. It was best that the children remained at the same house and location. They would not have to move or attend a different school. Such a change might worsen their condition, especially for Lan at that time.

Now, when my ex-husband comes to visit the children, I accompany him when he takes the children out, since three autistic children are difficult to manage and require constant care. At first, this was quite awkward for us, but eventually we learned to accept the situation and try to keep up the peaceful, happy family image whenever and wherever we are with the children. However, divorce can be like war, and all sides sustain losses. The children, especially, are the unwitting victims.

CHAPTER 13

THE AFTERMATH OF DIVORCE

– OVERCOMING OBSTACLES

The adage "What you don't know won't hurt you" may be applicable to my children. Nam and Mai did not understand much and, thus, did not seem affected by the divorce at all. Although Lan was an autistic eight-year-old girl at the time, her autism was less severe than the other two children, so she was more aware of the family situation. She was emotionally distraught when she learned her dad would be moving out of the house. She actually said to me, "Mom...Hurry up! We need to have another Daddy just like him...We need an exact copy of Daddy."

I replied, "I don't think so...I don't think it's possible."

She paused for a little bit, and then agreed, "You're right. Daddy is too big to fit in a copy machine."

At first she listened to her father and blamed me for everything to do with him leaving. It took me a while to explain to her, and it took her a long time to comprehend, the magnitude of the problems between us and the significance of our divorce. Eventually she understood and realized that while the family unit was getting smaller, my love for and bond with her and her siblings would never be broken; in fact, both were getting stronger. In retrospect, had I not proceeded with the divorce, she might not be where she is today — going to college and on her way to fulfilling her dreams...

During the next several weeks and months, I spent my time mostly on paperwork, household bills and maintenance, and the children's well-being and schooling. At first, I dreaded when something in the house stopped working, such as the garage door, the shower, the toilet, the sink, and so on. To save money, I even attended a few demonstrations at the local Home Depot to learn how to fix things. Eventually, I realized it would be less stressful and less time-consuming to have a professional handle the repairs. However, with a tight budget, I tried to fix minor things around the house and only called the professionals when I needed major repairs done.

Although I tried to keep a positive attitude, the divorce seemed to both scar me and scare me. I didn't think I could ever marry again. When I told a friend, "I already locked my heart and threw away the key," she amusedly responded, "Did you make a duplicate first?"

I had mixed emotions the day I received the Notice of Judgment from the court that officially ended my marriage. When the kids were at home, I plunged into my duties of caring for them so I would have no time to think about my life or myself. When my children were in school, I had some time to clean up and work on household chores. It was then that remnants of my 15-year marriage followed me wherever I went, especially when I passed by my ex-husband's room.

I thought about 15 years of being with someone that I never really loved. I thought about all those years that he was there, but he was not there. I cared for our children all by myself even when I was sick. Now that it was over, I was supposed to be happy, but I was sad. I thought, *I wish I had never met him. I wish I had met someone else who loved and cared for his wife and children, autistic or not. I wish I had met someone who made his family his number one priority. It will take some times for the bitterness and sadness to go away; after all, they say, "time heals all wounds."*

As the years went by, with all the chores and challenges, with all the setbacks and successes, with all the heartaches and headaches, I got used to being a single mom raising three autistic kids. In fact, I really embraced it as the highest honor that someone up there felt I had the qualifications to be chosen for such a job. A combination of daily routines and structured activities seemed to help us become more productive, efficient, and less stressed. Adding to the relief was the easing of Nam's crying episodes, indiscriminate chewing, and self-stimulation during this time.

In the morning I would brush all the children's teeth, give them their medication, and prepare them for school. I had to do a lot more for Nam (dressing, grooming, toileting, diapering, packing lunch, writing notes to the teacher, and so on) than for the two girls. After seeing Nam off to the bus and taking the girls to school, I usually cleaned their rooms, washed clothes, tidied up, bought groceries, and prepared that day's dinner.

I've always stressed the importance of cleanliness and personal hygiene, even when the kids were much younger. So, when they came home from school, they all had to take showers before eating snacks or doing homework. I would give Nam a shower first, and then I helped Mai with her shower. Lan could take a shower alone.

After feeding and playing with Nam, I would put him in his room for a nap. I then joined Lan and Mai at the kitchen table to help them with their homework or anything else that they needed assistance with. Mai did not understand much; thus, she asked for help with all of her homework. She always started by saying, "Raise your hand," and then she raised her hand to signal that she needed help. She was very messy in her work, especially in her writing (she held the pen or pencil in an unusual way). After finishing her homework, she would have a snack and then return to her room to take a nap, watch TV, listen to music, or play on the computer. I checked on her occasionally just to be sure that she was not "in her own world," repeatedly rocking, laughing, or talking to herself. I would also give her some extra math or reading practice problems, but she rarely completed them.

I prepared dinner for each of them separately because they had different tastes and preferences. Mai usually had dinner way before Lan and ate late-night snacks. If Nam woke up early from his nap or did not want to take a nap, then I had to focus on him while juggling to help my daughters. He usually vocalized, "eeee..." or roamed around finding things to chew or self-stimulated by repeatedly poking a spot on his hand, arm or face or by sucking his thumb. At times, he came to the bathroom and turned on the water faucet or shower and played with the water. Several years ago, he still even played with the water in the toilet bowl, but with medication, constant prompting, and behavior modification, that behavior diminished, and has not returned. It took much longer to help Lan and Mai with their schoolwork while caring for Nam. The juggling never seemed to end.

After Nam woke up from his nap, I would take him to the bathroom and then begin fixing dinner and feeding him. While feeding, showering, or dressing him, I also repeatedly prompted him to remind him of certain self-help skills.

Lan would work diligently for a while, only stopping briefly for a snack or dinner and bathroom breaks, and resumed working again. Sometimes, she got frustrated and cried. Then I had to stop everything and explain the concepts to her using simple terms and household examples.

At night, I brushed their teeth again and prepare them for bed. I had to get their school clothes ready at night because Lan and Mai would get agitated in the morning if they could not find a particular article of clothing. They preferred to wear the same familiar clothes; thus, I often washed and cleaned them the night before or I bought extra similar pairs. Gradually, they began to wear a variety of clothes to school.

Even now, my children don't always eat or sleep at the proper time. Nam has a tendency to wake up in the middle of the night or take long naps and go to bed late. Lan and Mai usually go to bed quite late. However, I tried to give them as much of a regular or structured routine as possible. Sometimes, I had a babysitter watching them while I ran out to do some errands. Initially, a trip anywhere with all of them would be quite exhaustive. With planning and preparation, our trips became less stressful, and we actually had fun with our weekend outings: driving leisurely around the neighborhood, stopping for ice cream, or getting a few things from the supermarket. Lan and Mai also enjoyed going to the Whole Foods market near our house because they both liked the bakery items and the free samples.

Nam started a class at Westmont High School County Program for the Severely Handicapped and was given a one-to-one aide. The teachers and staff there were wonderful and dedicated to their students. Nam's crying episodes seemed to taper in frequency and intensity while there, but he was still not improving significantly in other self-help aspects.

It took a while, but Lan began to adjust to my divorce and her father living in New York. It also helped that he called and spoke to Lan frequently, and he also made an effort to visit the children briefly on some weekends and special occasions.

Lan completed her fifth grade at Blossom Hill Elementary School and started sixth grade and eventually seventh grade at Fisher Middle School. She enjoyed choir performance. She was nominated Student of the Month in sixth grade and choir president in seventh grade. She really enjoyed learning and helping other students, especially those who were in a similar situation. Academically, Lan was doing much better, although I still had to check her homework and help her with math, science and reading comprehension every day.

Despite her academic success, Lan continued to experienced major problems with social interaction, especially in any group project or in a group setting. When there was a group project, Ms. J. or I had to speak to the teacher, and the teacher either gave her an individual assignment or put her in a small group of students whom she knew and who knew her. At home, Lan also struggled with persistent, repetitive questioning. When she asked me something, and I replied, "I don't know," she got upset. "How come you don't know? How come you don't know? I asked you a question. How come you don't know?" If I went to the kitchen, she followed. If I went to the living room, she followed me to the living room and asked the same question, repeatedly. "How come you don't know? How come you don't know?"

If I just answered anything to get her to stop, she said, "But that's not the right answer." If I asked her, "How do you want me to answer your question?" or "What is the right answer?" then she would get more upset.

"You know the answer!" she would scream as loudly as she could.

I tried everything I could possibly think of to reduce this repetition and fixation, but nothing seemed to work. At times like this, I needed to maintain my sanity. Sometimes I would just step out of the house or go to the garage and pretend to get something so she would have time to calm down. Other times, I asked her to go into her room and listen to music to reduce her anxiety, obsessive behavior, and impulsivity.

Sometimes Lan would be in her own world and repeat words, phrases, or events in the past (not pertinent to the situation at hand) over and over again. I found that if I could break this pattern or get her attention onto other things she would snap out of it at least temporarily. I said, "Lan, look at me. There is an exam coming up, and if you don't take time to practice, you will not do well." Sometimes I would mention the name of a person or person(s) who she was afraid to upset. "Lan, guess what. Your father (or sometimes Ms. J. or Mr. C.) just called and he (she) wanted you to start doing your homework or reading the next chapter in your book." Then I placed the book in front of her. I found this worked well.

There were times she had problems understanding the material given to her at school, and I read with her and tried to explain to her using simple terms, simple examples, and even using simple items around the house as models (a glass to illustrate opaque or transparency, a birthday hat to calculate the volume of a cone, oil and water to illustrate miscible properties and non-polar and polar compounds, chopsticks for parallel lines and angles, sugar and water to illustrate saturation, a ball to illustrate the concept of circle and sphere, etc.). She really liked mnemonics as a way to remember things, and I would scout my brain for these. Lan was so happy when I showed her some clever ways or short cut to arrive at a solution. Every time she finished any of her homework problem sets or her reading and writing assignments, I always encouraged her, "I knew you could do it! I am so proud of you."

Lan did not like interruptions, and many times she got upset that I had to interrupt teaching her to care for her brother, Nam, or her sister, Mai. She complained, "Mom, you love my brother (my sister) more than me..." I tried to explain to her why I had to stop and care for them, but it did not work.

I would make her write twenty times: "I am supposed to love and care for my brother (my sister) because..." or "If I continue to complain about my mom's caring for my brother (my sister), then I will lose the following privileges..." or "I am not supposed to ... because..." on a piece of paper and post it on the wall. Over the years, we had plenty of those papers. Before guests came into the house, we pulled those papers down and put them away in a box. After the guests left, we taped them back on the wall. It took her a long time, but she eventually realized that her brother and sister had more severe ASD, and they needed more attention. Upon her high school graduation, she asked me to throw those papers away since we no longer needed them.

My younger daughter, Mai, had a different type of behavioral problem at school: talking to herself repeatedly and laughing uncontrollably. For a while, she would answer "yes" to every question asked of her. One time, I showed her a picture of an animal, a cat, and a picture of a woman. Then I asked her, "Am I a woman?"

She said, "Yes."

I asked her, "Am I a cat?"

She also responded, "Yes."

She also had problems differentiating between "You" and "I." When I asked her something like, "Did you have fun at school?" she responded, "You have fun at school." If I asked her why she liked doing something, she simply responded, "Because you like it." Although we tried to correct this, and over the years there were significant improvements in her verbal skills, she continued to have problems with pronouns and reasoning.

As Mai gained more vocabulary, she began to talk inappropriately and in gibberish. At school, she talked to herself, used inappropriate words and phrases, and laughed uncontrollably. She also tore her homework and posters or pictures on the classroom walls. She could not mainstream with other children for a while because of her disruptive behavior. Because her behavior was getting worse, eventually she was transferred to Saratoga Elementary School Special Day Class.

At home, sometimes she fixated on certain inappropriate activities such as peeling paint on the wall, removing pieces of a tile from the bathroom floor, and tearing pages of a book. I would explain to her, put her into a different room, and work with her on more appropriate activities. She would eventually come back to doing the same thing. Mai also began fixating on using scissors impulsively. She used them to cut anything including her hair, clothing, papers, posters, and homework. One afternoon, I was badly hurt because I tried to remove the scissors from her hands while she was cutting her brand new dress. In retrospect, there were many times I have suffered cuts or bruises trying to prevent my children from accidentally hurting themselves. At that time, I had to hide all the scissors we owned, including student scissors. The only time I would bring a pair of scissors out was to work with her on behavior modification. With medication (Luvox, Prozac), constant prompting, and behavior modification, the frequency of her gibberish outbursts, disruptive behaviors, and inappropriate fixations seemed to abate.

As she gained a better understanding of language and improved in her behaviors, I was also able to help Mai more. One time, she was withdrawn to her own world and repeating things, laughing, and talking to herself. I knew she was afraid of flying bugs, such as bees or moths, so I tried to alleviate her fear and, at the same time, tried to bring her back from her own world, by saying, "Mai, look what I've found — a nice and tiny moth." Immediately, she turned around and said, "Where? Where's the moth?" Instead of feeling afraid, she became interested.

As a parent, I noticed that even though my children were all diagnosed with autism, from mild to severe, they didn't exhibits the same symptoms or features on ASD. The features that they all seemed to have in common were echolalia, repetitive behaviors, short attention span, and impairments in social interaction. Many of their autistic features also appeared at different chronological ages.

As mentioned previously, Nam, my first-born son, was — and continues to be — very severely autistic with mental retardation. He was slow in cognitive, language, social, and communication development. He did not express interest in being around other kids or playing games with them. Even though he had a significant delay in speech and language, he was able to say several words and a couple of short phrases by the age of two. However, as he got a little bit older, he lost whatever language or vocabulary he acquired and became nonverbal. He also started to cry more often and this behavior eventually escalated to what we called crying episodes — crying aloud and banging his head. Most of the time, he repeatedly vocalized unintelligible sounds or made self-stimulatory noises such as "eeee."

He also did not play with toys appropriately or meaningfully. Many times, I taught him how to play with a toy car, but he always turned it upside down and became fascinated with repeatedly rolling the wheels. When presented with a toy, he either chewed it or twirled it repeatedly. He was also echolalic, a poor sleeper, and rocked a lot. His eye contact was inconsistent. Sometimes he would look at me when I called his name, but other times he glanced elsewhere, even though his hearing tests were normal. He also had a short attention span and was unable to complete even a simple task unless someone was sitting there with him and constantly reminding and redirecting him. He did not want to cuddle that much and preferred to be by himself, sometimes staring at the light or at the wall. He could not point to any object and displayed repetitive hand gestures (bent his fingers in a strange way).

Lan's autistic features appeared quite differently than Nam's. Her verbal/language track was on the fast side when she was young. However, she had difficulty with eye contact and social interaction. In the early years, she was afraid of looking directly at my face. When I spoke to her, she looked at the floor or at a corner of the wall. At times, she had trouble expressing her feelings and understanding social cues and jokes. For years, group projects and activities were quite difficult for her. In the early years, she was afraid of any type of change, even minor ones: new blankets, new sheets, new environments, new people, and new situations. She also had many phobias; she was afraid of rain, wind, fire alarms, loud noises, sirens, snoring, cameras, camcorders, etc. She also exhibited obsessive interests: Eeyore, Barney, Arthur, Lemur, dogs, puppies, pets, and cats. Sometimes, she was in her own world and repeatedly said something not pertinent to the current situation. Lan was a picky eater, but Mai and Nam are not. In fact, she could not even stand the smell of certain foods, such as eggs, sausages, hamburgers, hot dogs, fried chicken, egg rolls, and spring rolls, and would become agitated if she smelled the aroma. Mai and Nam did not have this problem.

Mai had significant delays in speech, language, and communication development at first, but she gradually improved and gained them over the years. When she was very young, like Lan, Mai became upset if there were changes in her routine, although her fear of change significantly diminished as she grew older, whereas for Lan, these fears simply became less pronounced. She was also afraid of the wind and rain, but to a lesser degree than Lan. Mai has certain inappropriate fixations, enjoyed doing one activity repeatedly, and only reluctantly changed when prompted or redirected to something else. She put things in a straight line but did not get upset when things did not line up the way she wanted. She has always walked on her tiptoes. Lan did not have similar fixations, line things up, or walk on her toes. Although Mai's eye contact and social interaction were a bit better than Lan in the early years, sometimes when I talked to Mai, she would avoid direct eye contact, looking down or elsewhere rather than at me.

Mai's social interaction has improved over the years, but she still has tremendous problems interpreting social cues or making friends. As she gained more language, she also became more echolalic. Many times, she was in her own world; she talked and laughed repeatedly to herself. In school, she would say gibberish words, phrases, or things not pertinent to the situation repeatedly. Sometimes, she would laugh uncontrollably and disturbed the classroom. Lan did not exhibit either the laughing behavior or the gibberish talk. Mai answered every question the same way and for a long time, had trouble differentiating between "You" and "I." When I asked her, "Why did you tear your homework?" she responded, "Because you tear your homework." At fifteen years old, she still had significant difficulty with reading comprehension. She would read a simple three-sentence paragraph and have no idea what the paragraph was about. She would constantly rock back and forth in a chair. I can't recall how many chairs I replaced due to her rocking. Lan has never rocked repeatedly. Mai can help with a few light household chores, but Lan showed a clear aversion to doing any household chores. On the other hand, that trait can be attributed to the teenage years as well.

One interesting thing to note is that my children do not interact much with each other, even when they are seated at the same table, ride in the same car, or do a group activity, such as play a game or pass the ball to each other. They are aware of each other's presence, but, to a large extent, it seems that each remains in his/her own world or each has his/her own comfort zone that does not include the others. Lan occasionally would complain to me when her brother took her food or made a mess in the bathroom. Nam obviously was nonverbal and had little interaction with his sisters, and continues to be so. When the girls were young, possibly because of Mai's delay and limited communication, they rarely talked to each other. Now they can talk and share things, but they only do so if I initiate or encourage the conversation and the social interaction.

Over the years, however, I noticed that they do love and care for each other. One day, we were driving when they became hungry and looked for food in the car. Normally, I stocked my minivan with practically all the essentials: clothing, diapers, baby wipes, pillows, blankets, food, and drinks. The kids apparently had eaten all the stocked snacks on previous trips, except for a small package of crackers, and I had not had a chance to restock them. Usually, I had to remind Lan to share food with her brother and sister. I did not have to say anything that day. Lan opened the package and shared with them even though she said, "Mom, I'm *very* hungry." I also noticed this sibling bonding at other times. For instance, when Lan or Nam became ill, Mai was concerned, "What you eat?" or "You go doctor," she would say. I can only hope that this sibling bonding will be long-lasting, and that they will be there for each other in the future.

CHAPTER 14

A NEW BEGINNING – BACK TO SCHOOL

Although I tried to be strong and keep up the happy family image, there were days that everything that could go wrong went wrong. At times, the smile on my face just could not mask the tracks of my tears or hide the pain and fatigue.

One particular morning, after dropping my daughters at school, I drove around the neighborhood aimlessly. I thought of driving uphill near the mountain top and simply screaming my lungs out. I decided against this idea because most of the rich people lived up there, and they might call the police and put me in jail for disturbing the peace.

Instead, as I drove around, I asked God/Buddha to give me some guidance. I approached the corner of a big boulevard with multiple lanes, and the streetlight turned red, so I stopped. At the intersection, I saw a man in a wheelchair, trying to push his way across the street. The pedestrian light was flashing and eventually turned red, but he was still in the middle trying very hard with his hands to move his wheelchair to the other side. The streetlight turned green, and a few impatient drivers in the back of the line of cars started honking, but most of the other drivers were patiently waiting for him to cross. He finally made it to other side.

All of a sudden, I looked at my hands on the steering wheel and looked at my foot on the brake pedal. *I still have two hands and two feet, and here I am feeling sad and sorry for myself.* It was like someone had just splashed cold water on my face. It's cold but also refreshing, rejuvenating, and shocking. *I must do something positive and meaningful to make me happy so I can be with my children for the long haul,* I thought. *The road is long and the mountain is high, and I must be healthy mentally and physically so I can sustain and overcome the daily challenges.*

I started volunteering at my children's schools; it brought me great joy and personal satisfaction. School had always been a good sanctuary for me, so I thought about going back to school. Although I also loved being an engineer, after so many years staying at home with my kids, my knowledge, degree, and experience were definitely obsolete. Ever since my children were diagnosed with autism, I desired learning more about health sciences. So, I registered for a class at local community college, West Valley College. There were not many courses available because the semester was about to start and the registration deadline had passed. In addition, I had to pick a course that did not interfere with my children's pickup and drop off time. I was able to register for Contemporary Biology; however, I had to petition to add another course, Human Biology. The next semester I took Cell Biology and Organic Chemistry the semester after that.

I was amazed at how much I enjoyed school again and how interested I was in learning about the health sciences. I also loved to stay after class and talk to my instructors. In one of our conversations, my dedicated and caring professor, Dr. B., suggested I might want to consider advancing to professional school or graduate school. I replied that I would think about it.

One day, while waiting in a long line at the pharmacy pick-up counter, a vision crossed my mind. I saw myself as a pharmacist working to discover the cure for autism so other individuals and families could be spared the heartbreak. I also visualized being able to improve the health of patients and offer some relief to the parents of children with special needs. After this, I continued to take all the pharmacy prerequisite courses except for Anatomy and Physiology, which I had to drop due to conflicts with the children's schedule.

It was quite interesting that I came to West Valley College to find solace, but I actually enjoyed myself and discovered a new purpose in life. My instructors at West Valley College inspired me and helped me see that I could, indeed, find a new path for myself beyond my children.

It was not easy going to school and taking care of my kids at the same time. There were times I had to miss class because Mai had behavior problems at school or I had to do make up exams because my children were sick. One time, I was on my way to calculus class, and the school called saying I needed to pick Mai up because she was being extremely disruptive in class. I could not find a babysitter at the last minute, so I asked my instructor if I could bring my daughter to class. Since there was no quiz that day, he agreed. She sat next to me in the front of the class. A girl sitting next to me gave her a pen to draw on a piece of paper. However, as soon as my instructor began lecturing, she shouted, "You want to draw..." She stood up and wanted the marker from the instructor's hand. The instructor later told me that it was best not to bring her to class. I begged him just one more time after that when again I had no choice but to bring her or miss class.

Even though I had returned to school myself, I made a commitment to always assist Lan with her schoolwork first and ensure that all her homework was completed correctly and on time. She had begun seventh grade at this point. It was a tremendous effort to help her, as well as my other two children, but that effort has been reflected many times over in Lan's educational progress.

Another time I was on my way to take a statistics exam, when my son's school called and said he had diarrhea, so I need to pick him up. With his thumb sucking and indiscriminately putting objects in his mouth, diarrhea was quite common. Then my daughter's school called, too, because she was having behavior issues, and I had to pick her up as well. My statistics instructor was very strict — no make-up exam unless you were sick with a note from a doctor or you were in the hospital — and the make-up exam would be much more difficult. Thus, I had no choice but to call him. I asked if he could bring the exam outside to the handicapped parking spot where I parked the car with my two children inside. I tried to explain my situation and fortunately, he agreed. When he brought the exam outside, he looked inside, said "Hi" to the kids. To me he said, "Did you remember to bring your calculator?"

"Yes, I did," I said. "Thanks so much for understanding." I added.

"Good luck," he said before leaving the parking lot. After changing my son's diaper and giving him some Pedialyte, I began to focus on the exam. I also lowered the window a bit since my air conditioning unit did not work properly. While I was taking the exam on the steering wheel, my son began his "eeee's" and rocked the car continuously; my daughter repeatedly laughed and talked gibberish. I gave her a coloring book, but she refused to color. She also didn't want to play with her favorite toy or eat a snack. Then she got bored and began to shred the paper towels from our emergency earthquake bag in the car. She threw these rolled up shreds out the window. She also opened the boxes of baby wipes and discarded the wipes out the side window as well. Several students passed by and curiously peeked inside, but I just ignored them and focused on the exam.

When I finished and turned in the exam, I noticed the white pile of paper towels and baby wipes next to my car. I immediately cleaned them up. I was one of the lucky few who got a perfect score on that exam — despite the distractions in my car.

While taking Organic Chemistry, I had to hire someone to care of my children because the lab schedule coincided with Lan and Mai's pickup time. The caregiver was a very nice woman who was also the mother of a very good friend of mine at West Valley College. She really cared for my children, and we enjoyed having her company.

One time I had to bring my daughter to my English 1A class; amazingly, she remained in her seat most of the time. Many times, I attempted to take Anatomy and Physiology — the two remaining prerequisites for pharmacy school, but the labs were early in the morning, and I could not find any babysitters to come at that time.

I began to look for pharmacy schools in or near the West Coast. Many schools in California required pharmacy experience and carried stringent prerequisites, which I did not have. Then I came across a school located in Henderson, Nevada, that had an accelerated three-year program and did not require pharmacy experience. I applied to the University of Southern Nevada. It did not matter to me to what school I applied because I was more concerned about whether or not I could complete the program. In retrospect, I never saw a dull moment in handling college and children; I knew I would just have to be doing it in a different location, and perhaps, in unconventional ways.

CHAPTER 15

PHARMACY SCHOOL

– HOPE AND HARD WORK

If I could pin point one year of extreme stressors, it would be 2006. I had just gotten accepted to the University of Southern Nevada (USN) College of Pharmacy in Henderson, Nevada, but I had to complete the two required prerequisites, Anatomy and Physiology, in the summer prior to the fall start of school. In addition, I had to prepare for our move and find a place for us to live while going to school there. I asked my mom and sister to help me find a place in Nevada. At the same time, I had to get our current house ready either for sale or for rent. Our house was not in a good shape, so I decided to refinance and take out a big chunk for college tuition as well as for fixing the house in Los Gatos and finding a new place in Nevada.

My mom and sister went to Nevada to see a few of the houses for rent, but they were not in a good neighborhood or location. I decided to buy one in a good neighborhood and close to good schools for my children and me. I also had a company that came and replaced all the windows in our current house because they were old and broken. The kitchen and the bathroom were also remodeled. The boyfriend of my good friend actually helped us a lot in removing junk and clearing up our Los Gatos house.

105

Every day, I had to do labs, take quizzes, and study an entire chapter for each course. So, in the middle of the hot summer, I was taking two challenging summer courses, fixing the house, caring for my kids, and boxing up our belongings to prepare for the move. I also was trying to purchase a house and register my kids for school in Nevada. Since my kids were in special education programs, I had to contact the district there, send them IEPs, and check out available programs before registering them.

The summer courses went by quickly. While my children were asleep, I dived into my schoolwork. One night, I stayed up late to do an exam. I had my back against the window, and all of a sudden I saw a reflection of yellowish light come through the window glass. I thought someone was shining a flashlight toward me. I turned around and peeked out the window. There was no flashlight. It was the sunrise. I realized I had stayed up the whole night and, surprisingly, I was not tired.

As for the house in Los Gatos, I first intended to sell it, but Lan wanted to come back to the house in which she grew up. Thus, I put the house up for rent while we were in Nevada. We came back to the same house in Los Gatos during my third year of pharmacy school in 2008, which were all experiential rotations.

I finished all the final exams just a couple of hours before the mover came and packed the computer. The mover was a good friend, and he (and his friend) helped us a lot with packing and transporting our things to Nevada.

The transition was quite difficult, especially getting my children registered for schools. Finding schools for Lan and Mai and getting proper services (in their IEPs) were not as difficult as finding the right school and the right service for Nam. Things did work out eventually for Nam. In the meantime, my fast-paced pharmacy program had already started.

In my first year of pharmacy school, I was able to hire a babysitter, who had come from California. She seemed like a nice lady. However, in many respects I still had to take care of my children because she could not speak English well, and she did not want to drive. The children would usually go to school early in the morning and come home around mid-afternoon. She stayed with the children when they returned from school until around 9:00 p.m. every day. Lan and Mai attended Greenspun Middle School. There was no program for severely autistic children at Green Valley High School so Nam was sent to Del Sol High School. During this time, I also started to work at Walgreens and continued working throughout my third year.

The first several weeks, Lan cried a lot and wanted to go back to Los Gatos. Mai did not cry that much, but she had behavioral issues and focusing problems. Nam was in a class of higher functioning autistic students and, initially because of the lack of staff, he would come home with soiled diapers and clothing. Eventually, the school did provide a dedicated aide to help with his hygiene and safety.

Within a few months, Lan adjusted better to the new environment. Choir also helped her gain confidence and social skills. I was so proud when she was chosen Student of the Month. It was also amazing that she won the Geography Bee at her school and represented her school in the State level competition. I asked her geography teacher, Mr. M., to take Lan to the competition, because I was pressed to complete a project at school. I later joined them when she made it as one of the top ten finalists; however, she did not win the title to represent her school in the National Geography Bee competition in Washington, D.C.

The next year, Lan started at Green Valley High School while Mai still remained at Greenspun Special Day Class. Mai's teachers, aides, and staff in Special Day Class helped her tremendously in both academic and social development.

The babysitter returned to California after I completed my first year of pharmacy. In my second year, I was pretty much on my own, except for several weeks when my mother's friend, a nice and friendly woman, came to help. Nam continued going to the Autism class at Del Sol High School. The school provided Nam with the same dedicated, caring aide from the year before, and even though Nam did not improve much, he seemed content at school.

In the morning, I dropped Lan off at Green Valley High School and then drove to my pharmacy class. In the afternoon, she finished school around 2:30 p.m., but my class ended later; thus, she had to wait about an hour before I could pick her up. I told her to wait for me in the office, but she wanted to be with some of her friends and usually waited for me outside the school. Many times, I drove to school nervously to pick her up and then became worried sick when she was neither in the office nor in front of school when I arrived. She later explained that she was helping some of her friends in the Student Council with a project or she had to attend a club meeting after school. The school bus dropped Nam and Mai a bit earlier; fortunately, the State of Nevada provided a babysitter for one hour to care for Nam before I came home.

Overall, Lan flourished in her ninth grade year at Green Valley High School. In her dance class, she met a group of students that changed her life. In short, she felt that the small group of friends at Green Valley High School really welcomed and comforted her in times of need. Any type of change has always been difficult for her to adjust: new house, new school, and new environment. As a new student, she felt lonely, and they made her a member of their group. In her own words, she later described this experience, which I included in Appendix C. She also enjoyed performing at Choir concerts and even traveling to Hawaii for Choir competition. She had lots of fun and made a few new friends during the trip.

Academically, Lan also blossomed. She won a medal in the Science Olympiad state competition and represented her school in the National Science Olympiad in Washington, D.C. While earning straight A's in all her courses, she also took time for community activities. She ran relay races to raise funds for cancer research, participated in clubs after school, attended a few autism events, volunteered for Meals on Wheels, and volunteered at a local library. There were also challenging times in her biology class — not so much academically, but socially. I talked to her teacher, and we tried our best, but there were days when she felt left out and alone. Fortunately, she did have a group of friends who supported and comforted her. Some of them were a bit older than Lan, but they cared and comforted her and made her happy.

I had a hectic and exhaustive second year of pharmacy school. Looking back, I do not know how I juggled everything, and yet none of the balls was dropped. Even with a busy, accelerated pharmacy program, my children were still my top priority. I stocked up on their favorite food, and after class, many times I brought them their favorite treats. Weekends were usually reserved for grocery shopping and household chores. When Lan and Mai came home from school, I always helped them with homework or anything else they needed. Every day, I waited until my children would go to sleep and then I began to study. Sometimes I was exhausted and fell asleep right on my laptop. The keyboard beeping sounds awoke me occasionally. There were times I slept in my chair until it would tilt to one side and threaten to dump me right on the floor. Luckily, I woke up before that happened.

Then there were mishaps and unfortunate events. Without the help of babysitters for the children, even going to the emergency room for a minor medical scare was like an Olympic speed skating event. Rushing through medical care and rushing home late at night, I immediately removed my arm sling to prepare a school lunch for Nam, brush Nam's and Mai's teeth, change Nam's diaper, and prepare the kids for bed. The next morning, I woke up at 4:00 a.m. to prepare Nam and Mai for school and put them on the bus. Then I dropped Lan off at Green Valley High School before going to pharmacy school. I did not want to miss any day of school or exam. A day later, I took an exam, and, fortunately, I passed. (A passing grade was 90 percent or above).

Sometimes I had to miss classes due to the children's illnesses or the children's IEP meetings. One time, I got a call from Mai's school notifying me that she had fallen down in PE class and was complaining about her ankle. I took her to have an X-ray, MRI scan, and consultation with an orthopedic surgeon. Fortunately, she did not have to go through surgery.

Nam did have to go through surgery, though. He had an operation to take care of his wisdom teeth. During times like these, it seemed the very foundations might be crumbling — literally — under our feet. In fact, we discovered a leak underneath our house in Henderson, and we exhausted a small fortune to repair.

While our time in Nevada was definitely interesting, I admit I am relieved that period in our lives is over. Overall, except for several visits to the doctor, the children stayed generally in good health and adjusted reasonably well to the new environment. My neighbor, Mr. M., helped with the yard work, and occasionally he watched the children while I ran an errand or finished up an assignment at school. He was about the same age as my father, and like my father, was a nice and caring person. He told me he liked to drink coffee, and I brought him a cup of Starbucks coffee practically every day as a token of my appreciation.

I recall that I would call my dad in California each time I passed an exam at pharmacy school. He constantly reminded me to take care of myself because he knew too well that I always put my children's well-being first. He told me, "You should always take care of yourself first. Always try to better yourself; when you are getting better, your children get better." Other times, he recalled how, when he was only 6 years old, he worked as a manual laborer to support his family and later joined the army and escaped serious injuries in many perilous battles. He reminded me that his faith and his family sustained him through many of life's challenges. He told me that with faith, love, and hard work, I would sail through many difficult challenges in my life just as he did. These words kept me going when things felt tough.

I was deeply saddened when I learned in the fall of 2010 that my father had a rare and aggressive cancer called acute T-lymphoblastic lymphoma (T-LBL). While his body was weak, his mind was forever strong and determined. There are no words to express my admiration for his tremendous courage battling the enemies within. As of this writing, he has undergone a series of chemotherapy treatments, but the outcome remains uncertain and the prognosis is still poor. Our family is devastated. While we know time is not on our side, we continue to try everything for him, and we will always love and support him.

Having my dad's encouragement meant the world to me, especially at times when I wanted to give up. Having good fortune to encounter a good support network enabled me to keep my spirits up. At first, I really did not like going to USN at all. I thought about the impact of this fast-paced program on my children. *What if they need me and I can't be there for them? Will I be able to complete the program successfully given my difficult situation?* There were so many "what if's."

One professor on the staff, Dr. D., was aware of my situation, and he did everything he possibly could to help me with the transition. He reached out to another student who had an autistic child and asked her to contact me. He also helped me search for the proper schools for my children. I was a bit nervous at the beginning of the school year, and he gave me words of encouragement and inspiration. He was an amazing professor, a dedicated admissions staff member, and, most of all, a caring person. Attending the school was a lot of hard work, but in the end it was worth it. I was glad to complete my degree, and I was happy to have met so many nice classmates, professors, and staff at USN College of Pharmacy.

CHAPTER 16

THE RETURN TO LOS GATOS

After completing my second year of pharmacy school, I tried to get most of the experiential rotations I needed to complete my degree in San Jose, California, so I could return to our house in Los Gatos. Needless to say, Lan and Mai were happy to return to Los Gatos in 2008. The move two years before proved to be our test run, and we avoided most of the problems from the original move. The move back to Los Gatos was a little trying, only because I had such little time to pack, move, and register my children for schools. Our things were still in boxes when I had to report for my first clinical rotation, a specialty pharmacy located in Huntington Beach, Southern California, rather than in Northern California near our home. That summer, my children and I stayed temporarily at my mom's house in Southern California. My mother's friend, a very nice lady, came and took care of my children for several weeks while I worked at my rotation.

After that first rotation, my children and I moved back to our house in Los Gatos, and I continued with the remaining rotations. I started my second rotation with Dr. A., an internal medicine doctor, then off to my next rotation at Good Samaritan Hospital in San Jose. The night before starting my rotation at Good Samaritan Hospital; however, I had an accident. The next morning I showed up with cuts and bruises on my face. Nevertheless, I did not take any time off. After several weeks, the bruises finally healed, but I was left with a scar on my forehead. I finally completed my last rotations at Walgreens and O'Connor Hospital in San Jose. Although it was a lot of juggling and hard work, it was also such a learning and rewarding experience working at the various rotations.

By the end of my third year of pharmacy school, I was physically exhausted. I remember holding a cup of tea while sitting on the sofa one night, reviewing my notes for the licensing exam. I woke up in the middle of the night shivering and cold. The cup of tea had spilled on my chest while I dozed.

Lan began the tenth grade at Los Gatos High School (LGHS), and I enrolled Mai in Special Day Class at Fisher Middle School. Finding a school for Nam was a bit challenging because of his age and his severe autism; the best option for him was the Erikson School/Severely Handicapped County Program. Nam had a rough start at first but became accustomed to the program. In fact, all three of my children had problems adjusting to the change, although Lan was a bit more emotional than her siblings.

At first, Lan was happy to be back. She tried hard to rekindle her friendship with some of the girls at Los Gatos High School that she knew back at Fisher Middle School before the move to Nevada. Although most of the students were nice, some of the students knew her from Blossom Hill and already had formed an opinion of her. The stigma of autism followed her wherever she went. Others had already formed their own cliques and were reluctant to include new members.

There were days she came home really upset and cried because she felt that some students deliberately left her out or ignored her even when she just tried to be friendly and said, "Hi." Her case manager, Mr. H.C., was very understanding and helpful. At the beginning of the year, she participated in Speech and Debate and seemed to initially do very well and make some friends there. She even became a semi-finalist in one of the events. However, toward the end of the year, she felt sad and lonely in school and began to miss the group of friends she had spent time with in Nevada. She also felt sad because one student she knew passed away suddenly.

She compensated for her loneliness and her social problems by eating more and more. It was during this time that she began to gain weight, and her appearance did not help secure more friends.

Although I was busy with clinical rotations, I made it a priority to help her with her academic and social problems. Many times, I told Lan to focus more on her academic interests and hoping that it would take her mind off of the daily nuances of social gatherings and friendship. Eventually, she agreed. The summer of her tenth grade year, she was accepted to the Stanford University Education Program for Gifted Youth (EPGY). She had a hard time adjusting to the program in the beginning, but gradually she began enjoying her first college experience.

After going over the courses for her junior year, I realized Lan only needed two more courses during her senior year. Lan asked me if she could graduate early; thus, I spoke to the school counselor about that possibility. Combining the junior and senior years into one created major challenges, but in the end it was worth it. Thinking back, I don't think Lan ever had an easy school year. This year though, the social aspects of inclusion and friendship would trouble her all the more. As a reward for her academic success, she wanted me to take her out to eat more often. I wanted to emphasize eating healthy food, etiquette, and appropriate behaviors at a restaurant or in a public place, so I agreed. I also utilized this time to discuss our lives and my own college experiences as well as to prepare her for the college environment.

During Lan's junior/senior year, she grew fond of a stuffed animal cat named C., in Mr. P.'s U.S. government class. She told me that if she was having a bad day, hugging this stuff animal would comfort her more than anything else. Up to now, she is still very fond of this stuffed animal cat. She could also turn to her small group of understanding friends for solace and reassurance.

In the past, Lan never really liked economics and always dreaded the course. Every time I discussed an economics subject matter, even casually mentioned things like bills, mortgage or budget, she would cover both ears and tell me to stop. However, as a requirement for graduation, she had to take Economics. Perhaps it was fate. Her Economics teacher, Mr. C., was someone she really admired. Things changed. She would come home and tell me how Mr. C. made the course really interesting and enjoyable. She spoke very highly of him and how much she enjoyed being in his class. Mr. C. would come to always be an important person in Lan's life. For some reason I can't explain, there was a special bond, and he was, is, and will be like a father to Lan. He gave her advice, comforted her, and always encouraged her.

While Lan continued to do well at LGHS, Mai was also making moderate progress at Saratoga High School's Special Day Class. Mai started to use the computer to surf the internet for things she liked, such as contemporary songs and music, cartoons, and maps. I monitored her internet usage and occasionally took away her computer privileges when she refused to obey certain rules. Recently she has learned to write e-mails. Many of her e-mails are still not appropriate and in gibberish, but she has improved significantly in her vocabulary, grammar, and spelling. She also has finally used the pronouns "I" and "you" appropriately, with much less prompting and redirecting. She continues to sit in the chair and rocks repeatedly, and some of her fixations come back occasionally, such as using scissors to cut items indiscriminately. Sometimes she still impulsively blurts out inappropriate words or phrases such as saying "I love you" to a stranger she meets at the mall. She continues to need help in communication, comprehension, and social skills. The teachers and staff at Saratoga High School Special Day Class are very patient and understanding, and they work really hard to help Mai.

Nam seems to be contented with structured programs and activities provided by Beyond Potential Learning Center (BPLC) Adult Day Care facility. Although Nam needs constant supervision due to his severity in the ASD (nonverbal communication, lack of safety awareness, and personal hygiene), he really enjoys his time there and has fun doing activities with the staff. The staff at BPLC is also very patient and supportive. Recently, Nam has learned how to wave; he actually waved "hello" and "goodbye" to me!

CHAPTER 17

THE GRADUATION

AND THE REFLECTION

In retrospect, every year with my children posed challenges, but the early years especially so. As time went on, however, I saw tremendous progress, particularly with Lan. As she made great strides in her reading, writing, and overall academics, she began to ask more questions, especially about autism, and became more aware of herself, her brother, and sister. She no longer asked me why her brother could not talk or why her sister said gibberish things or rocked repeatedly. One day she even asked me if she could read her own IEP. She had come a long, long way.

In the past, she would come home from school upset or crying because no one wanted to be her friend, her partner in a group, or because someone teased her. She did not know why she behaved impulsively or repeatedly said certain nonsensical things or why other students had negative impressions of her and called her "weird." Out of frustration, one day she said, "Mom, I just want to be normal like all the other kids..."

"Then you work hard to overcome your autism," I said. "Tell yourself this: I have autism, but autism cannot have me... I can do it...Never, ever, ever give up..."

I also made her memorize my four rules of thumb, or rules of THINK, inspired by IBM's "THINK" motto: "THINK before you act. THINK about what you say before saying it. THINK about the consequences, and THINK of ways to better yourself." Even today, I don't know how she processed that information, but every day she demonstrated to me that she tries to overcome her autistic tendencies. And Lan's little steps have paved the way for the miles and miles of accomplishments she has achieved since she began her journey in this life.

Joining choir was probably the most significant event in Lan's life because it jump-started her process of overcoming social phobias. Although behavior modification and other methods also alleviated her fears, I believe another turning point in Lan's life came when she presented her speech, *M & M's – The Colors of Diversity*, in front of a large audience, and won first place in the Fisher Middle School Annual Speech competition. It instilled in her the confidence to overcome the communication obstacles and aspire to do greater things in life.

Looking back over the years, I could not imagine that Lan would have made it to or through elementary school, let alone graduate high school or attend college. Lan has blossomed into the well-rounded student with excellent academic achievement and social awareness. She has come a long way from the girl who was in her own world displaying most autistic characteristics that some thought would be impossible to overcome. She has worked so hard to triumph over the obstacles in her life and achieved so much that she amazes even her own parents. Although she still has a long way to go and some days remain more difficult than other days, she has always tried her best: academically, personally, and socially. I have never believed that she was "cured" of autism, but I know that she is inching closer to becoming a productive, independent individual and hopefully, she can live a close to normal life.

As mentioned previously, my son and my younger daughter have more severe forms of autism. My son will always need constant supervision, and my younger daughter will need some supervision. As time goes by, it is my hope that my younger daughter,

Mai, will acquire adequate practical social and communication skills that enable her to live more independently and with a reasonable amount of help.

In many respects, however, I have seen moderate to significant improvements over the years in both Nam and Mai. No one could have imagined the day when Nam would stop his crying episodes and sit still in the car or the bus for a short trip. His indiscriminate chewing of non-food items and his self-stimulation has also been reduced over the years. His personal safety and hygiene, however, continues to be a major concern. No one could have imagined the day Mai could talk, read, and write, although her speech, reading comprehension, and writing are way below her age group. At this point, she continues to have significant problems with reading comprehension and still has echolalic tendencies and certain fixations, as well as the occasional gibberish episodes, but she has come a long way.

Nam and Mai may never be at the same function level as Lan, but I accept them and love all of them equally. Each child is different and, like any child, progresses at his or her own pace.

I noticed that my children, especially Lan and Mai, benefited from a structured environment and regular daily routine. In general, if they *trusted* the environment and were *comfortable* with the routine, then we gingerly could expand this environment and routine and gradually introduce new or a bit more advanced things into it. I equate this to taking a new medication; you don't know if your body is allergic to the medication or how your body will reacts to the side effects, so you start out with a low dose and going slowly. Gradually you increase the dose if needed.

I also learned not to have too many expectations of them and to accept success as well as setbacks. Sometimes, I had to use external reinforcements for them, such as giving them treats or mentioning someone's name (that they don't want to upset) or adding a reward for a particular behavior or assignment. Using these methods with Lan, I have achieved reasonably good success. With Mai, sometimes these tools worked; sometimes they did not. With Mai, I have had to do more assessment to discover methods that work; it takes more trial and error.

When the children were young, I created a template algorithm to work with them (primarily with Lan and Mai) in terms of helping them with school work, improving their language comprehension, or improving their verbal skills and communication. The template begins with "PEA" then becomes PEAR or PEAS or PEAT.

P: Plain and simple (words/instruction/command).

E: Evaluate (observe how they process/absorb the information, how they associate the words with the action).

A: Assess (was the wording simple enough, did they understand it, did they get confused, did they get frustrated, and did they carry out the task correctly).

R: Repeat as necessary (repeat the words/command/instruction about 5-10 times). If it works, try the same thing several hours later or tomorrow to see if they remember. If they remember the instruction, then I expand/add/modify the instruction/command to include more words/multiple commands/instructions. If not, then go back to "PEA."

S: Stop (because they get frustrated/cried/screamed). Try again at a different time.

T: Trial and errors. (They did not get frustrated, but they appeared confused or did things incorrectly; substitute with different words/rephrasing, sometimes adding visual aids or enforcement with reward/food). Then go back to "PEA."

For Nam, I continue to make sure every day that his safety, health, and personal hygiene are my priorities: brushing teeth, toileting care, and reducing his indiscriminate chewing and "stimming." Even now, I have to help him with practically all of his personal hygiene and grooming. I tried to bring him to a barber not long ago, but Nam is unable to sit still. Therefore, to shave and cut Nam's hair by myself literally can take hours. It's not perfect, but I do the best I can. In the past, the schools and I focused on additional sign language for him. However, it seemed he did not associate or comprehend the difference between one sign and another, and his random hand gestures complicated the actual signing.

After his crying episodes subsided and eventually stopped, I focused on toilet training for Nam and reducing his self-stimulation. It has been a few years with some improvement, but I am still working on these skills as time permits. I'm also teaching him simple self-help skills, such as cleaning himself in the shower, putting his clothes on after a shower, cleaning himself after toileting, and washing and drying his hands. In the past, I also worked with him to reduce his frequency of chewing non-food items. Sometimes, I would teach him to follow a simple command, such as picking up or bringing me a familiar item, turning on or off the lights, opening or closing the door, etc. Sometimes, he did a good job with what I taught him; other times he just stood there.

Nam's disposition is so sweet and gentle that it was virtually impossible to be angry with him – slightly frustrated maybe, but never angry. I would love to teach him to speak someday, but I no longer expect miracles. I would rather focus on the reality than the dream. It's a blessing that Nam is never aggressive. In fact, all of my children are sweet and mild-mannered.

Sometimes, they also inadvertently bring me joy and laughter. I remembered one time Lan asked me, "Mom, what are you thinking? How come you're so quiet today?"

I sighed and replied, "Lan, the world has five billion people, but I don't even have a best friend…a companion."

She shook her head in disbelief and responded, "Oh, Mom. That's not true…The world is about seven billion people, and you've made a 30 percent error!"

When Lan was much younger, at the airport, she pointed to a man with a protruding belly sleeping soundly on the chair next to her, and asked, "Mom, is there a baby in the tummy?"

In one of her fifth grade assignments, she had to interview a parent, so she asked me, "Mom, what is your favorite color?"

"Lan, I don't have one favorite color, but I like black, blue...and purple," I said.

She said, "Mom, but those are the colors of bruises!"

Lan also has a tendency to be impulsive and loud. When I have taken her to a restaurant, bookstore, library, or any public places, sometimes she has blurted out loudly, "I need to pass gas," or "I need to go poop (or pee)." I tried to correct her by telling her to talk softly and reminding her to substitute her words with something more appropriate, like "I need to use the bathroom." It had not worked that well. I know that she likes mnemonics, so one day I coined a mnemonic for "Pass Gas and Evacuate," which we both now refer simply to as PG&E. (So sorry, Pacific Gas and Electric.) While out dining or in a public place, she would say, "Mom, you need to pay the PG&E bill *soon*," and that was a cue for her to be excused and go to the bathroom. That worked particularly well. Eventually she was able to interchange the mnemonic with just "I need to use the bathroom."

Mai has had some interesting moments, too. Before I would go grocery shopping, I usually asked Lan and Mai to write down a list of items to purchase. In particular, I wanted to teach Mai to write properly because her handwriting, spelling, and grammar were poor and messy. One time, Lan wrote a long list, but after searching and shopping at a few stores, I finished Mai's list but I could not finish Lan's list. I was tired, so I returned home. When Lan realized I didn't have all the items, she became upset. I told her, "Lan, you wanted everything on that list. Have you thought about me? It's now 2:30 p.m. What have I eaten? Zippo, Nada..."

Mai heard that and jumped in, "And I want to eat Zippo, Nada, too."

Around Thanksgiving I turned on the TV. A commercial showed someone carving and serving turkey. Mai immediately blurted out, "Can you have some?" as she approached the TV with open palms waiting for food.

Mai talked a lot about a girl with orange hair that she either had seen in a book or on TV. One day, she came out of the bathroom and told me that her own hair was orange. I did not notice anything different about her hair except that it was wet; however, as I came closer, I realized what she was talking about. Apparently, she had put orange juice on her hair to make it orange. Another day, I saw blotches of orange in her hair. I asked her what had happened and she told me she had painted her hair with orange crayons and markers.

Mai always had a field day with guests. They were frequently greeted with, "What color is your hair?" or "What year your house was built?" or "Are you a man or a woman?" She also repeatedly asked for their names even though they already told her many times.

Mai enjoyed listening to Vietnamese music and surprisingly, some of the songs she liked were also the ones I liked as a child, even though I never sang or listened to those songs with her. She also enjoyed listening to music by contemporary American singers and artists. A few American guests came over, and she actually tried to sing Vietnamese songs to them.

Nam had many poignant moments. When he was around eight years old, I was changing Mai's diaper but could not find the baby powder. I looked around and found Nam white from top to bottom. He had squeezed the entire baby powder bottle on his head, his face, and all over his body.

One night I woke up feeling cold and wet. I discovered Nam lying next to me laughing in his wet clothes. Apparently, he woke up in the middle of the night, turned the shower on, and stepped into it with his clothes on. Luckily, the bathroom floor is padded with large pieces of rugs and towels to prevent slipping. After that, I put latches on the bathroom door at night to prevent him from doing things in the bathroom that were dangerous.

In the middle of the night, there were times Nam would go to the kitchen, pull everything out of the refrigerator, and make a huge mess. I would see butter, cream cheese, and jelly all over his hair and his face in the morning. After that, we installed a baby safety gate on his bedroom door to keep him from roaming around the house at night.

At the age of eleven, Nam had a tendency to put things up his nose. One day, the babysitter told me Nam had found a crayon, broke it into pieces, and put some of them up his nose. I took most of the pieces out except for one stubborn piece stuck snugly in his right nostril. I did not know what to do so I tried mineral oil, and I even let him smell pepper to sneeze it out. None of these tactics worked. He did not sneeze, but I and the babysitter sneezed so much that we had tears in our eyes. Then I encouraged him to jump and hoped gravity would drag it out. He did not jump by himself so I jumped with him. I did this so many times that I was exhausted and lying flat on the floor. Eventually, this did, indeed, work.

One day, I let Nam sit next to me in the kitchen while I prepared his food and dinner. As soon as I turned around, he grabbed the peeled garlic and chopped onions and ate them all. He did not even have a slight squint in his eyes.

When I was studying pre-pharmacy courses at West Valley College, there were several times Nam chewed my homework. I was contemplating whether to tell my teacher "my son ate my homework," but I decided I would stay up late and redo all my homework instead.

When I was in pharmacy school in Nevada, one day I was so tired I brought my PowerPoint lecture to study in bed. The next morning I woke up and could not find the materials anywhere on the bed. As I looked down on the carpet, I discovered a pile of ripped and chewed pieces of lecture notes next to Nam's mattress.

I think about all those years of hard work, headache, and heartache. I think about all those years of tears and cheers — more tears than cheers — trying to help Lan with social adjustment, addition, subtraction, multiplication, division, algebra, geometry, reading comprehension, English, biology, chemistry, calculus, etc. I think about all those long evenings and late nights of scouting my brain for shortcuts and mnemonics, searching for things around the house to use as models, finding different ways to explain things to her, screaming my lung out so that she could grasp a particular concept. I think about all the moments of patiently calming Lan through her phobias, trying to reduce her echolalia, curbing her fixations or obsessive interests, and finding ways to reduce her repetitive questioning or impulsivity.

I also think about the days and nights of trying different methods to teach Mai to speak properly or to reduce Mai's gibberish and repetitive, impulsive, and disruptive behaviors. I think about many days of desperately calming Nam during his crying episodes, complete with head banging and bloody noses. I think about many nights of interrupted sleep due to his waking up in the middle of the night, wetting his bed, or making a mess in the bathroom, or running around and repetitively saying, "eeee..." I think about all the successes and setbacks of raising three autistic children while married, amidst the turmoil of a divorce, and alone after my divorce.

Yet, all these memories faded into oblivion the day I attended Lan's graduation from Los Gatos High School. The girl who tried so hard to fit in had begun to gingerly step out of her autistic shell and into the "real" world. That day, June 11, 2010, I was just the proud mom of a straight-A student who graduated a year early with honors and would be attending U.C. Berkeley. I felt the cooling breeze, the fresh air, the blooming flowers, the shining sun, and I actually tasted it and savored it — the fruits of our labor.

Then, after the graduation ceremony, I thought about the new challenges that Lan would face as she embarked on her college journey. I also thought about Mai and Nam, and the challenges and the daily juggling that would remain a constant in our lives. Nam's progress seems to have slowed, and he is still in diapers, but he seems to enjoy his time at the Adult Program – Beyond Potential Learning Center (BPLC). I realize my children still have a long way to go.

A year earlier, in 2009, I graduated with my pharmacy degree and completed my licensing. Perhaps I am passionate about using my educational and life experiences in a positive and meaningful way: working and helping other families of children with special needs in a non-profit organization, inspiring others to overcome the challenges and obstacles in their lives, raising autism awareness, giving advice to parents of autistic children who need more understanding with medications, and sharing my own story. I wanted Lan to know that in any difficult situation, any difficult challenge, if she is dedicated and resilient, she can succeed. If she wants a role model, she does not have to look very far. In a way, as I completed and fulfilled my vision with graduating from pharmacy school, it was now Lan's turn to start out on her own journey. She has already endured so much in her life, and I will be there for her now and in the future to see her to her dreams as well.

The thought of writing a book about my life and sharing my story did cross my mind at various times in the past. However, that thought had to be relegated to the back burner to give room for the more urgent and pressing priorities of my life as I knew it. For many years, the prospect of a full six hours of sleep at night or of a night out at dinner and movie just simply eluded me. After finishing with my degree and helping Lan complete her high school years, I saw an opportunity to take a break and to put my thoughts and experiences on paper. Also, for the first time in my life, I finally had an opportunity to exhale. It seemed I'd been holding my breath for as long as I could remember.

Writing this book was definitely an amazing and cathartic experience for me. In the process, I cried tears of joy and tears of pain as I relived my life and traveled down memory lane. I finally could let go of the heaviness and heartache that had weighed me down thus far. At times, I was afraid if I didn't write my story now, I might not have the chance, the courage, or the memories to write it later, especially with my age and my children's situation.

With autistic children, you become accustomed to taking one step at a time, one task at a time, and one day at a time. You also become stronger and more resilient. You welcome each unexpected challenge as an opportunity to learn and to grow. Your children teach you a lesson in courage and patience you could not find in any school or any textbook. With each parental accomplishment or accomplishment of your children's, no matter how big or small, you inch closer to the finish line, yet the finish line always remains in the distance. You learn to accept and to assess — to accept your children's ability as well as their disability. You learn to accept successes as well as setbacks. You assess many trials and try many things. You learn to smile even if there are tears in your eyes and a lump in your throat. You learn to be content with what you have and not to compare to what others have. You learn that there will be stormy weather at times, but the clouds will soon clear, and the sun also rises. You learn that there are many red lights ahead, but they soon turn green. You learn to use the compass of love to find your children and bring them back. In short, you learn a valuable lesson in love, acceptance, and perseverance. At least, that's what raising three autistic children taught me.

EPILOGUE – A FINAL THOUGHT

I am fortunate to have a home, although if these walls could talk, they would tell you it's not much of a home; it's more like a place of existence. I am lucky to live in a country where there are good school districts with caring and supportive staff and county programs that helped my autistic children in those early critical years. Although I had to work hard to earn everything in my life, including a job and an education, I was glad that I had the motivation and the dedication to do it over the years. I also was blessed with the love, strength, and perseverance to care for my children in the past, and hopefully, for many years to come.

I thought about all the women and men in every corner in the world, especially in rural, poor, underdeveloped, poverty-stricken areas, who are raising their autistic children all by themselves with little or no help and support from any programs or from anyone. I wonder if they can withstand the barrage of small town gossip, criticism, and stigma, and even the blame for their children's disease. At best, they probably stay with relatives and keep their children home most of the time, afraid to let them be seen by others. I wonder how many severely autistic children are labeled by their community as crazy, weird, psychotic, mentally retarded, or even possessed, only to be sent away to a sub-standard institution with lack of nutrition, basic care, and education.

It is my wish that this book will inspire people facing any challenge in their lives. In particular, I wrote this book for the parents and caregivers in the United States and all over the world who face similar situations like mine and for the individuals who unfortunately are struck by autism and may not have the opportunity to voice their basic human rights, concerns, or shape their future. I hope in some way it will bring inspiration and positive changes to their lives and their children's lives. I also hope it will spark additional research and innovative treatment programs for a disease that is rampant and painful, yet remains a mystery decades after it was first discovered.

For me, I know the road is still very long, rough, and bumpy, but somehow, I feel like "the little engine that could." It is my desire to be there with my children to help and support them for as long as I can. By writing this book and sharing my story, I have opened old wounds and relived the sadness and sweetness of memories. There can never really be closure to the profound pain and stigma, but I learned to live, to cope, and to move forward.

With no previous experience and no set of instructions, I have learned as much from my children as they did from me, and we will continue to learn and grow together. I am not perfect; however, as a single parent, I have raised my children over the years with all the love, caring, and compassion I could possibly give them.

Sometimes, looking into the mirror, I nod my head and think, *that little girl did not get lost at sea. Through the turmoil and turbulent tides, she found her way home…That little girl has finally grown up.* And this was her story.

APPENDIX A

TEN MOST FREQUENTLY ASKED QUESTIONS

I would like to use this opportunity to address the ten most common questions posed to me over the years.

Frequently Asked Questions

1) *Why did you have two more children knowing that there is a possibility of having another autistic child?*

After reading the book, I think it's clear to everyone. According to Dr. K., the Vermont Child Development Clinic Developmental Pediatrician, the result of Nam's fragile X syndrome was negative, so I was told it was okay to have more children. Lan, my older daughter, did not appear to have prominent symptoms of ASD until her toddler years; by then I was already pregnant with my third child.

2) *Could it be that the children imitate each other?*

It's a misconception that since they are in the same household, the children simply imitate each other. This could not be farther from the truth. My children have a variety of different signs and symptoms in the ASD spectrum, and the onset of each was unique to each child.

3) *How did and do you do it — take care of three children with autism?*

If I don't, who will? In short, if you love your children, you will climb the highest mountain, endure the most arduous journey, accept some of the harshest criticism, and find your own ways through many loneliest and darkest of days. Yet, somehow, it's all worth it. You always hope and believe that tomorrow will be better than today. I would add that, reading and understanding more about autism helped me tremendously. Also, with autistic children you always have to plan way in advance, hope for the best, and prepare for the worst. There is just no easy way to put this in context.

4) *Why don't you move closer to be with your parents and siblings?*

I thought about that when my children were quite young. However, at that time, it seemed that I would place tremendous burdens on my parents, physically and emotionally. My siblings have their own lives, and I hate to bring any additional burden to anyone. Now that my children are older, I may think about that possibility.

5) *Is it true that you raised all of them with no physical and psychological support from anyone?*

Unlike other families with autistic child or children who have a support system with families, friends, and relatives around to help them, I was all alone. I wish my husband had been my support person, but it did not turn out that way. Although he helped financially, it was quite a challenge to care for my children all by myself. The county programs helped with some supportive services.

6) *What seemed to work for you over the years?*

It's hard to pinpoint just one thing, one event, or one person. There are many contributing factors, but I would say the unconditional love for my children is what enabled me and continues to enable me to carry on over the years. Also, a structured and regular routine provided us with the template from which we could modify as needed. I make it a habit to plan ahead of time. I always have essential things in my car for my children, and it reduces the hassle and anxiety when travelling with them.

It's not easy, but I tried to instill in my daughter, Lan, the values that I live by: caring, compassion, and kindness. I want Lan to know that having autism is a positive attribute since it will strengthen her and empower her to overcome obstacles and do good things in life. It almost seemed like a blessing in disguise.

There were days when everything seemed to go wrong, and I had to take a step back and look at the big picture and remind myself of the positive things that I have. I made it a point not to focus on what might have been, but instead to focus on what I have now. I also reflected on the caring people that touched my life and my children's lives, the sweet memories that cherished my heart, and the words of wisdom from my father and my teachers, and somehow they brought comforting feelings.

Music has always been a close companion to me, and whenever I am feeling a bit down, music brings a soothing feeling to my soul. At times, singing a song in the shower also helped erase all the negativities of the day. It seems trite to mention, but after a shower I usually have this rejuvenating, refreshing feeling, and a renewed hope.

7) What methods or medication seemed to work for your children?

To a large extent, I believe a combination of medication, constant prompting, and behavior modification worked reasonably well for my children. Also, it is not just one-size-fits-all, and it's not just a simple method or assessment. Although I don't have names for all the method/methods that I've been using to help my children over the years, the PEA, PEAR, PEAT, PEAS method has achieved reasonable successes.

You have to know your child thoroughly: what he/she can or cannot do, how he/she absorbs/responds to what you would want him/her to absorb/respond, and design/modify a method that works specifically for that child. You continue to repeat/modify/fine-tune until you are satisfied with the outcome or until you reach their limit, physically and psychologically. Bringing my daughter to her friend's house or a playgroup helped improve her social skills tremendously.

My children tried many medications before settling on Prozac (fluoxetine). Prozac seemed to reduce many of their autistic features. To this day, they're still taking Prozac. I know it's hard but every parent should monitor their children's medication, progress, and setbacks, and see what works for each of them. What seemed to work for my children may not work for yours, and what seemed to work for one child does not necessarily work for another child. You should work closely with your children's doctor. I strongly recommend trying one medication at a time and not multiple medications at one time.

8) *What do you want to tell other parents who are currently facing or may face similar challenges?*

Don't give up! You can do it! For those who agonized over the questions of "Why?" and "What could we have done?" perhaps it's best to leave those questions behind or to leave them with the professionals; you have to keep your sanity and move on. We all belonged to a club that none of us wanted to join. I am sure that all of us would do anything not to be in the situation we are in right now; yet we have neither the time nor the energy to focus on what might have been. Our membership is secured, and we have to make the best of what the club offers.

Before we attempt to heal our children, we must first heal this gaping wound in our hearts. We must rise to the challenge and live above all the negative criticism. It's a long, arduous journey, and we must be strong physically and psychologically.

I think one of the hardest decisions is whether or not to tell your friends or other people about your children. It took me a while, but I finally came to the conclusion that it's best to be open and honest about the whole thing. The first time I told my friend about my situation, I felt like a heavy load was lifted off my shoulders.

9) *What were some of the common comments that you hear over the years? Were they mostly positive or negative?*

It depends. Some people, especially those who believe in karma, superstition, and reincarnation, told me I must have committed sins or done many bad deeds in my last life to be in my situation. I wish I could have gone back to my last life and corrected whatever it was that I did. Other comments questioned the validity of my children: "Are you sure you did not adopt them?" At public places such as malls, restaurants, and supermarkets, a few people told me that I did not discipline my children the right way; some suggested a "good spanking" to control their repetitive behaviors or stimming vocalization. Still, others were puzzled, "Did you take any medication during your pregnancy?" "Did you smoke, drink alcohol…eat raw meat during pregnancy?" "Did they fall and hurt their heads?" "Did they have high fever after the vaccinations?" "When/Why did they all become autistic?" "Did they eat something really bad for their brain?" "Did your family or his family have a genetic disease that you didn't know?" It was a long time ago, but I remember a woman telling me she was afraid her children would be like mine if her children played with my children, even though I told her that autism is not contagious. There were also many positive, supportive comments, "You are a good mom…Don't worry…Things will be okay," and words of encouragement, like "Hang in there…I am so proud of you."

10) *What would you have done differently?*

I love my children and have no regret having them in my life. They mean the world to me! I only wish my children could have a father who makes his family his number one priority. Although I tried all I could to help all my children, I still wish I could have done more for my son and that there were more programs available decades ago to help him.

APPENDIX B

A DAY IN THE LIFE

As recorded in my journal, these recollections offer a glimpse from a typical day.

February, 2009 (time frames are approximate)
6:00-7:00 AM

Wake up, brush teeth for Nam, Mai. Wake Lan up as well. Get Nam's and Mai's clothes ready. Put diaper on for Nam and pack his lunch. Feed Nam breakfast if time permits. Put lunch and diaper in backpack, write note for teacher, and get Nam ready for bus. Get myself ready for pharmacy rotation at O'Connor Hospital. Give all three of them medication (Prozac). Remind Lan and Mai to put homework/books/folders in their backpacks. Lan would be extremely upset and agitated if she forgets her schoolwork at home. Give Lan and Mai their lunch money.

7:00-7:15 AM

Ms. J. is here to take Lan and Mai to school.

7:15-7:20 AM

I leave the house, heading to my rotation.

3:30-4:00 PM

Pick up Mai from Fisher Middle School, then pick up Lan from Los Gatos High School.

4:30 PM

Nam comes home. Take off his clothes/diaper; brush his teeth, give him a shower, and then give him a snack. Pick up dirty clothes from his backpack and wash. Read note from Nam's teacher. Lan and Mai both take a shower after coming home from school.

5:00-6:00 PM

Prepare dinner, wash/dry clothes, clean the children's rooms, kitchen/bathroom, wash dishes.

6:00-8:00 PM

Dinner/feed Nam. (Lan and Mai don't eat at the same time or the same kind of food. They have different preferences, and Lan has taste aversion to certain food). After giving the other children their dinner, I work with them on their homework/projects. Nam made a mess in the bathroom. Clean up. Bring the trash out.

8:00-10:00 PM

Continue to work with Lan. Mai asked for help with homework and finished her homework quickly but messy. Mai returned to her room to watch cartoons or listen to music and rock on the chair. Check on her to make sure she's not in her own world laughing and repeating things inappropriately. Give Mai's medication since she is still has runny nose and cough. Nam is in his room self-stimulating "eeee..."/ sucking his thumb/running around. Took Nam to the bathroom 3 times already. Nam took off his clothes and wanted to shower, again (he signaled by turning the water on). Lan is getting frustrated with her homework and is crying. Focus on teaching her the easy way to approach it. Follow the PEA, PEAR, PEAS, PEAT method. She felt better but kept on repeating, "Why did Nam interrupt while you're helping me? You like my brother more than me..." Tried to explain, did not help. Make her write 20 times, "I will not get upset when my mom has to care for my brother because..." but it did not work this time. She went to her room and listened to music for about 30 minutes and was much better when she came out.

10:00 PM-12:00 AM

Brush teeth for them and prepare them for bed. I took a shower then checked mail/voicemail, pay bills, checked e-mail from my children's teacher. Work on my rotation assignment. Add extra items to the grocery list and post on the refrigerator door. The bathroom sink is clogged, I need to fix it.

12:00 AM-3:00AM

The children don't sleep right away...I continue to work on my rotation assignment while watching them.

APPENDIX C

THE CHILDREN'S HIGHLIGHTS

Here are some of the highlights and events chronicling each of my children's journeys.

Nam Nguyen

- Born in 1988, Burlington, Vermont, 9 lbs. 3oz.
- Sat alone at 6-8 months
- Spoke first word at 12-14 months
- Crawled at 9-11 months
- Walked at16 months
- Spoke short phrase spoken at 2 years old
- Diagnosed: 1992
- Nonverbal; severe communication and social impairments; short attention span; lack of focus; unable to attend to tasks; no peer playing; put practically everything in mouth; played with toys inappropriately; unusual finger/hand motions; stimming; rocking and repetitive behaviors; echolalia (prior to loss of language); frequent crying episodes; inability to interact with others.
- Currently: 23 year old, nonverbal, non-gesturing, attends Adult Day Program, still wears a diaper, and needs constant supervision.

Schools

- St. Francis Pre-School/Essential Early Education, Burlington, Vermont, 1992

- The Children's Annex Autism Special Day Class, Kingston, New York, 1993-1996
- Cherry Chase Elementary School/Special Day Class, Sunnyvale, CA, 1996-1998
- McKinnon Autism School/Severely Handicapped County Program, San Jose, CA, 1998-1999
- Hazelwood Elementary School/Severely Handicapped County Program, San Jose, CA, 1999-2001
- Dartmouth Middle School/Severely Handicapped County Program, San Jose, CA, (2001-2002
- McKinnon Autism School/Severely Handicapped County Program, San Jose, CA, 2002
- Castro Middle School/Severely Handicapped County Program, San Jose, CA, 2002-2003
- Westmont High School/Severely Handicapped County Program, Campbell, CA, 2003-2006
- Del Sol High School/Autism County Program, Las Vegas, NV, 2006-2008
- Erikson Special Ed/Severely Handicapped County Program, San Jose, CA, 2008-2010
- Beyond Potential Learning Center/Severely Handicapped Adult Program, Milpitas, CA, 2010-present.

Lan Nguyen

- Born in 1993, Poughkeepsie, New York, 8 lbs. 8 oz.
- Sat alone at 5-6 months
- Spoke first word at 10 months
- Crawled at 9 months
- Walked at 11 months
- Spoke short sentence/phrase at 15-18 months
- Diagnosed: 2001
- Easily distracted; lack of focus; lack of social pragmatic skills; unable to interpret people's feelings, social cues or jokes; impairment in social interaction skills; impulsivity; repetitive behaviors; echolalia; avoids eye contact; obsessive

interests; afraid of changes (even minor ones); obsession to maintain sameness; saying things inappropriate for current situation; fearful of certain items and certain noises.

- Currently: freshman at UC Berkeley/class 2014. Still has social challenges, needs help with reading comprehension and social interaction.

Schools

- Growing Footprints (Pre-school), Los Gatos, CA, 1998
- Blossom Hill Elementary School, Los Gatos, California
  - Special Day Class/mainstream class,1998-2000
  - Mainstream classes with aide, 2000-2004
- Fisher Middle School, Los Gatos, California, 2004-2006
  - Mainstream classes with assistance as needed
- Greenspun Middle School, Henderson, Nevada, 2006-2007
  - Mainstream classes with assistance as needed
- Green Valley High School, Henderson, Nevada, 2007-2008
  - Mainstream classes with minimal (as needed) or no assistance
- Los Gatos High School, Los Gatos, California, 2008-2010
  - Mainstream classes with minimal (as needed) or no assistance
  - Graduated from Los Gatos High School 2010
- UC Berkeley undergraduate freshman — class of 2014
  - UC Berkeley DSP/DSRP providing assistance as needed

Mai Nguyen

- Born in 1995, Poughkeepsie, New York, 8 lbs. 9oz.
- Sat alone at 7 months
- Crawled at 12 months
- Walked at 14 months
- Ran without falling at 24 months
- Toilet trained at 6 years old

- Spoke first word at 24-26 months
- Spoke first short phrase/sentence at 6 years old
- Private Speech therapy at home 2 hours/week with Ms. CJR, Los Gatos, CA, 1998-2000
- Diagnosed: 2000
- Severe communication deficits; speech and language delay; significant delay in expressive and receptive communication; delay in self-help skills; poor social interaction; prefers same routine or structure; lack of focus; short attention span; delay in cognitive skills; impulsive at times; echolalia; laughing uncontrollably; repeatedly says gibberish; disruptive behaviors in the classroom; rocking and repetitive behaviors.
- Currently: attending Special Day Class at Saratoga High School. Needs help with all aspects of academic, behavioral, and social skills.

Schools

- Mooreland Discovery Schools Preschool/Special Day Class, San Jose, CA, 1999-2000
- Blossom Hill Elementary School, Los Gatos, California, 2000-2004
    o Special Day Class/a few mainstream classes with aide
- Saratoga Elementary School, Saratoga, California, 2004-2006
    o Special Day Class/a few mainstream classes with aide
- Greenspun Middle School, Henderson, Nevada, 2006-2008
    o Special Day Class/a few mainstream classes with aide
- Fisher Middle School, Los Gatos, California, 2008-2009
    o Special Day Class/a few mainstream classes with aide
- Saratoga High School, Saratoga, California, 2009-present

o   Special Day Class/a few mainstream classes with aide

Below is an excerpt of the letter that my daughter, Lan, wrote about Mrs. P., the former principal of Blossom Hill Elementary School.

...Several years ago, I was just a third grader at Blossom Hill Elementary School and you were the school principal. As a child with autism, I had trouble with communication and social interaction. I told you that my hobbies are singing and listening to music. Thus, you suggested that I join Choir to alleviate my fear of people's faces and loud noises (hand clapping, sirens, etc.). You even gave me rides to choir practices since my mom has to care for my severely autistic brother and sister. Choir has already started but you talked to the teacher and convinced her to give me a chance – a chance of a lifetime.

...What a difference Choir made in my life! What a difference you have made in my life! At first, joining Choir was very hard for me. Gradually, I was able to look into people's faces and carry on a close to normal conversation. I am no longer afraid of the hand clapping sounds or loud music. I love to perform on stage and enjoy singing at every Choir concert. Best of all, I also make a few friends. Even on a busy schedule, you were willing to go the extra mile for me. You took the extraordinary step that few principals have taken. I admire all that you have done to help my family and me. Sometimes we opened our door and saw a package of spelling books or mathematics. My mom thanked you but you brushed it off, saying that they were old books and you just wanted me to use them for extra practice. I have learned so much from you and I truly appreciate your caring and kindness.

Below is an excerpt that Lan wrote about her experience at Green Valley High School in Henderson, Nevada.

SEPTEMBER 28, 2007
One month had passed and I haven't made many friends like I planned on doing. I was soon losing hope. Dance PE first period my

classmates didn't recognize me from previous years, hence it took time to get along with everyone. Choir I always got nervous even after we introduced ourselves the first day. The only person I was able to find was a girl named Carly. She, this day, played the most important role in leading the way to joy, faith, and courage. Not only has she begun my journey through high school, but she has guided me in choir and outside of school.

It was that day after coming out of Dance PE frustrated at a misunderstanding I walked to choir and Carly asked what was wrong. Luckily we had a substitute so we didn't miss anything the first twenty minutes. Two choir leaders were teaching the class for the day. One of them I looked up to since I came into the choir. She had the biggest personality that can light up a room in an instant. Her name was Kylie. May it be that I will be this kind of person one day...I prayed. To start with, I had to get to know her, but I was always shy in the choir. While Carly and I were talking, she advised me to see one of the choir leaders. The other choir leader was our section leader; she, too, was very productive and efficient in keeping things together. Her name was Julie. She, too, played many supporting roles this year.

Carly then decided that Kylie would help me with these things so she then told Kylie to see me. As I paid for my pasta dinner tickets for a choir concert, a hand touched mine. "Lan will you please come over..." I turned around and saw that Kylie was asking for me outside. My heart beat faster than the rate of the trombones in a 6/8 time next door. For a while, we conversed about what happened until we were chatting about the best things of life as though we were best friends all along. She then assigned me three tasks to help me improve my social life: 1. Meet Ariel, her best friend. 2. Attend the choir party on Friday. 3. Meet at least five people every day.

The choir party was a huge success, probably one of the best choir parties I have been to. Many people asked me if I was the girl Kylie spoke of...

...Everyone is at some stage in becoming successful with what they want to do with their life. The hard truth is, not everyone will get what they want. There are those out there who don't have what they need because of certain circumstances we are not normally aware *about because we are focused on our own wants. It is a main reason why human nature can be cruel. Lies, bullies, misconceptions, hatred, and war root from human nature. Along with attaining success we help others do the same because nobody alone can make the world perfect. This is a self-explanatory concept called love. Compassion is a step branched from love when we assist those that are in need. There are many positive changes we want to see in the world; it takes the courage, faith, and confidence to make it happen. Maybe human nature is not too cruel as long as we discover the best of ourselves. No matter how hard we try to hide ourselves, someone out there is always seeing us through. If we be ourselves then shall there be peace because we know one another so much that we bring happiness altogether?*

I have "graduated" from the place called experience. I have earned my diploma, gown, and cap already...they aren't here yet because young as I am, there's still more to discover. Currently, this feeling of overwhelming shock and sadness has quenched my soul. Honestly, I feel lucky to mature early and my next wish is to help others who are fighting battles in their life. The next step takes more than time and patience; it's about keeping inspiration because life is so valuable that you don't realize something is meaningful until it's gone. Many of you in my life have inspired me to be a better person every day. I wish the graduating class of 2008 a bright future; I will never forget the way many of my friends this year made me feel. For the class of 2009, 2010, 2011 and so forth: always continue to stay important as you are because you are the new generations of the world.
Love,
Lan

Below is an excerpt that Lan wrote about her 10th grade experience at Los Gatos High School in Los Gatos, California.

The Year in Reflection
By <u>Lan Nguyen</u> on Monday, May 25, 2009 at 9:55pm

First of all, I want to say thank you to friends, many who are far away, for keeping in touch with me and giving me so much encouragement to be the best person I can be and much better...

...Where to begin tends to be the most difficult part on reflecting the end of the year. This year, especially, has been a tumultuous one filled with ups and downs, multiple in-betweens, and moments of joy and reflection complementing hardships and trials faced. Upon attending high school in the place where I grew up the first time in so long, I was off to a new start. It was going to be a great opportunity to challenge myself academically and to fulfill those dreams. Grade wise, this year was the best year. I could not feel more proud of my accomplishments than I already am right now and I am happy that I had the chance to keep up with the standards I set for myself and many more goals to come. I want to continue working very hard because these achievements will only linger with determination, cooperation, and a sense of exploration.

If you do not know me well enough already, I have Autism, a mental disability which affects communication and social skills. The disorder may also affect one's ability to process learning and information in some cases. I am one of the few who have the chance to work in a mainstream classroom, travel various places, including Hawaii and Washington DC, and can socialize reasonably well, if not the best I can do. There are many people out there, even those who don't have the disability, who long for this kind of self-fulfillment and experience, and I hope that they have the opportunity soon to do so. My brother and sister are more severe in Autism than I am. Even though it may be difficult coping with trying to keep the family together, I am nonetheless grateful that I have a single supportive mom and a divorced hardworking father who have been guiding us through multiple walks of life...

The following is an excerpt from Lan's speech, *The Hero within You,* at the 2008 Miller Cup Speech Competition at Los Gatos High School and later at the Individual Event Speech competition at Milpitas High School.

...The heroes of my life have shaped me in so many ways that I would not be the person I am today without them. My parents were told from the doctors and professionals that I had autism, a neurological disorder in which there is no cure. In 2007 the Centers for Disease Control and Prevention concluded that "the prevalence of autism had risen to 1 in every 150 American children" and about 1.5 million are living with the autism spectrum disorder. I did not understand what autism was or how it will affect my life later on. Communication and social events were the biggest and most challenging obstacles. Any changes, certain noises, and certain equipment would terrify me. Unable to communicate coherently and easily distracted, I felt isolated at school.

Words could not convey what my mom went through. Despite being single with three autistic children, she never gave up on us. She taught me many lessons but the greatest lesson was that I can overcome autism. In one IEP meeting, there was a principal, Mrs. P, who suggested that I joined choir to improve my communication and social deficits. She actually picked me up every choir rehearsal because my mom had to care for my siblings. Ms. J took me out of the classroom when I broke into meltdowns or said things inappropriately. She would find different ways to help me express my feelings instead of crying. Then there are many teachers, aides, case workers, psychologists, and counselors who helped me when I needed assistance. Then there are a few friends who comforted me when someone told me I was "weird". Over the years, I have decided that I have autism but autism cannot have me. Autism affects communication but it is not a communicable disease so it's OK to lend a helping hand. I needed help and there were people who lent me a helping hand. These are ordinary people who made a difference in my life; they are my genuine heroes...